Children on the Trail

A Child's Spiritual Formation Guide for Churches and Parents

SANDRA J. SUTHERLAND

CHILDREN ON THE TRAIL
Copyright © 2022 by Sandra J. Sutherland

All rights reserved. Neither this publication nor any part of this publication may be reproduced or transmitted in any form or by any means, electronic or mechanical, including photocopying, recording or any information storage and retrieval system, without permission in writing from the author.

Unless otherwise indicated, all scriptures taken from the Holy Bible, New International Version®, NIV®. Copyright © 1973, 1978, 1984, 2011 by Biblica, Inc.™ Used by permission of Zondervan. All rights reserved worldwide. www.zondervan.com The "NIV" and "New International Version" are trademarks registered in the United States Patent and Trademark Office by Biblica, Inc.™ Scripture quotations marked MSG are taken from THE MESSAGE, copyright © 1993, 2002, 2018 by Eugene H. Peterson. Used by permission of NavPress, represented by Tyndale House Publishers. All rights reserved.

Print ISBN: 978-1-4866-2299-3
eBook ISBN: 978-1-4866-2300-6

Word Alive Press
119 De Baets Street, Winnipeg, MB R2J 3R9
www.wordalivepress.ca

Cataloguing in Publication may be obtained through Library and Archives Canada

Advance praise for *Children On the Trail*

Children on the Trail presents a valuable resource for our churches. Drawing from decades of experience and wisdom, Sandy's writing is a valuable resource that emphasizes the importance of meaningful relationships and good teaching. The most important responsibility for our generation is the spiritual well-being of the generation that comes after us, and *Children on the Trail* will help our churches discern next steps to care for our children.

Children on the Trail reminds us that faith is a lifelong journey that begins in childhood, and churches and families share the responsibility for the path our children choose. Sandy helps us understand the needs of children at different stages in their lives, and how we can support the growth of faith in their lives. The Trail is not simply a guide for children's ministry but an inspiration to help us prepare for forming faith in our youngest generations. It helps a church imagine how it can best come alongside their children and point them towards Jesus. I highly encourage you to read this book with your ministry team and commend it as a valuable tool.

—Dan Pyke
Director of Youth and Family Ministries
Canadian Baptists of Atlantic Canada

Drawing on her years of ministry experience in Atlantic Canada, Rev. Sandy Sutherland has compiled this practical tool for both paid and volunteer ministry leaders within the church. This book lays a foundation to equip those who minister with children. I have had the opportunity to draw on and share Sandy's wisdom and vision for the Trail in preparing leaders for Next Generation Ministries, and I believe it is a good example of seeking to lead with clarity, purpose, and direction. It is a valuable resource, and I am thankful that Sandy took the time to put this together so many more can benefit from her knowledge and insight regarding this important ministry within the church.

—Jody Linkletter
Lecturer, Next Generation Ministries
Associate Director of Doctoral Studies and
Academic Assistant to the Associate Dean
Acadia Divinity College

Children on the Trail is a comprehensive resource for churches to develop an intentional approach to children's ministry. I am excited to have this excellent resource to recommend to churches responding to Jesus's command to let the little children come to Him. The book encompasses the important principles of a lifelong discipleship journey. Forged from years of study, experience, and expertise, Sandy Sutherland offers churches today a proven approach that is adaptable, customizable, and achievable.

—Tanya Yuen
Children and Family Ministries Associate
Canadian Baptists of Ontario and Quebec

To my own Andrew and Laura....
once children on the Trail,
now trailblazers for the children in their lives.

Contents

	About the Trail	ix
	The Start of the Trail	xiii
	About the Trail Guide	xvii
	Why Children and Children's Ministry Are Important	xxi
	Children and Spiritual Formation	xxvii
1.	Welcome: Trail Section One	1
2.	Wonder: Trail Section Two	11
3.	Discover: Trail Section Three	23
4.	Launch: Trail Section Four	47
5.	Forging the Trail	65
6.	Safety on the Trail	69
7.	Recruiting Trailblazers	73
8.	Parents on the Trail	81
9.	Partners on the Trail	89
10.	Building the Partnership	95
11.	Digital Expressions of the Trail	101
12.	Grandparents on the Trail	107
13.	Immersing the Trail in Intergenerational Ministry	113

Appendix 1: Ceremony of Promise and Blessing	119
Appendix 2: Principles for Godly Parenting	125
Appendix 3: Sample Child Protection Policy	129
Appendix 4: Larry Richards's Seven Principles for Effective Role-Modelling	137
Appendix 5: Helping Parents with Discipline	139
Appendix 6: Helping Parents Nurture Good Relationships with Their Children	145
Appendix 7: When a Child Wants to Be Baptized	151
Appendix 8: Recommended Resources	163
Bibliography	175

About the Trail

When Eugene Peterson named his book *A Long Obedience in the Same Direction*, he could have had the Trail in mind.[1] Loving God and becoming more like Jesus is a progression that can begin at birth and continue for a lifetime.

The Trail is a visual depiction of that spiritual journey. There is a deeper track that opens off the Trail, a track forged by longing for God and marked by intimate experiences with Him. But on the way to that grace-activated, deeper, and more intimate experience with God, we nurture the first stages of a relationship with Him on the Trail.

A series of signposts divides the Trail into sections by age groups and gives each section a name. Spiritual formation in each section of the Trail is matched with age-appropriate cognitive, physical, emotional, and social development. This is what makes the spiritual goals and concepts suitable for each age group.

When someone begins their faith walk later in life, they are taught the initial spiritual concepts as a foundation for all that is to follow. The developmental goals of the Trail are meant to be cumulative; each person adds to their spiritual understanding and practices as they mature.

The Trail is a resource for churches and parents. Please see the following graphic.

---

1 Eugene Peterson, *A Long Obedience in the Same Direction: Discipleship in an Instant Society* (Downers Grove, IL: InterVarsity Press, 2021).

The Sections of the Trail

AGES 0–2
SPIRITUAL GOALS AND OUTCOMES

- God made me
- Jesus loves me
- Church is a happy place to be
- Church is a family for my family

AGES 3–4
SPIRITUAL GOALS AND OUTCOMES

- God made everything
- Jesus is my best friend
- I can talk to Jesus anywhere, any time, about anything
- The Bible is God's special book

AGES 5–8
SPIRITUAL GOALS AND OUTCOMES

- I can trust God
- Obedience is best
- Giving is God's way
- I treat others the way I would like to be treated

AGES 9–11
SPIRITUAL GOALS AND OUTCOMES

- Understand adolescnce
- Choose Jesus
- Begin Spiritual Disciplines
- Serve others

AGES 12–14
SPIRITUAL GOALS AND OUTCOMES

- Find God's whats and whys
- Choose good influences
- Be a good influence
- Discover my gifts

AGES 15–17
SPIRITUAL GOALS AND OUTCOMES

- Put God first
- Listen for God's voice
- Actively share my faith
- Serve God with my gifts

AGES 18–25
SPIRITUAL GOALS AND OUTCOMES

- Honour God with my choices
- Passionately share the love of Christ in word and deed
- Pursue accountability
- Practice Godly stewardship

AGES 26+
SPIRITUAL GOALS AND OUTCOMES

- Grow with Spiritual Disciplines
- Give finances and other resources
- Care for others
- Reach and teach successive generations

The church can use the Trail to design spiritual nurture for every age group, parents can use the Trail to design spiritual nurture for their children at home, and the church can clasp hands with parents along the Trail to form a dynamic partnership of spiritual formation for children and youth.

Note that the Trail was inspired by the spiritual pathway Brian Hayes developed with Legacy Milestones at Kingsland Baptist Church in Katy, Texas.[2] The Trail section names Wonder and Discover, along with some of the spiritual goals for these age groups, were borrowed from *Think Orange* by Reggie Joiner.[3]

---

[2] Brian Haynes, *Shift: What It Takes to Finally Reach Families Today* (Loveland, CO: Group, 2009).

[3] Reggie Joiner, *Think Orange: Imagine the Impact When Church and Family Collide* (Colorado Springs, CO: David C. Cook, 2009), 154.

The Start of the Trail

Like so many things, the Trail was God's answer to panic and prayer. I had just become the children's pastor at West End Baptist Church—now called The Crossing Church—in St. John's Newfoundland and wanted to be sure that the children's ministries I led were making a spiritual difference in the lives of the children.

I knew it would be easy to simply entertain the children at church, or even just provide quality childcare. I was used to serving up a potpourri of Bible stories and lessons to kids, merely hoping that something would hit the mark. But I felt there had to be a much more effective approach to children's ministry and a way to evaluate what we were doing.

Then I read George Barna's book, *Transforming Children into Spiritual Champions*.[4] It transformed me into someone who wanted to champion children, the church's ministry to and with children, and the church's ministry to and with parents. Barna helped me rediscover the principles of children's ministry I had learned while earning my master's degree in Christian Education at Gordon-Conwell Theological Seminary in Wenham, Massachusetts. He also helped me revisit intentional ways in which parents can nurture their children spiritually.

---

4 George Barna, *Transforming Children into Spiritual Champions: Why Children Should Be Your Church's #1 Priority* (Ventura, CA: Regal, 2003).

One of the books we studied in seminary was called *The Intentional Family*, by Jo Carr and Imogene Sorley.[5] I don't recall much about the book, but I've never forgotten its title. My husband and I had tried to be intentional parents when we were raising our own children, but throughout my many years in church ministry I didn't see other church leaders teaching parents to be intentional. So I didn't teach and lead that way either.

Then I read Barna's book, and I knew I had to make some courageous changes in my ministry.

The Trail was inspired by the spiritual pathway Brian Haynes developed called Legacy Milestones at Kingsland Baptist Church in Katy, Texas. I read Brian's book *Shift* and fell in love with the way that church built a partnership with parents around specific celebrations on their pathway:

1. The Birth of a Baby
2. A Child's Commitment to Christ
3. Preparing for Adolescence
4. Commitment to Purity
5. Passage to Adulthood
6. High School Graduation
7. Life in Christ[6]

But I wanted the church and parents of young children to have a reason to come together more often and more regularly. I also wanted to identify specific age-appropriate goals the church and parents could work on together for the child's spiritual formation.

The Trail, like Legacy Milestones, became a progressive pathway, a continuum of spiritual growth and development for a

---

5 Jo Carr and Imogene Sorley, *The Intentional Family* (Nashville, NY: Abingdon Press, 1971)
6 Haynes, *Shift*.

lifetime, but we divided it into age group sections so we could assign each section its own spiritual goals.

At first, I called our new path the East Coast Trail, after our famous and beautifully groomed coastal hiking paths in Newfoundland. It was my colleague Rev. John Campbell's idea to shorten it to the Trail. I loved John's suggestion. Right from the start, I felt that God had given us the Trail not just for our church in St. John's, Newfoundland, but for all our churches in Atlantic Canada. Well-groomed hiking trails are part of the DNA of our scenic provinces.

While I was working on the first sections of the Trail, Rev. John Campbell, the youth pastor at West End Baptist Church in St. John's at the time, named the Explore, Experience, and Emerge sections and drafted an original set of goals for these. We worked together on Invest, the adult section of the Trail. Later, while I was pastor at First Moncton, my colleagues and I revised some of the original goals.

When I first began to think about recording my thoughts about and experiences with the Trail, I knew I couldn't do justice to every section. It was John Campbell who suggested I write only about the first four sections—Welcome, Wonder, Discover, and Launch. These are the ones I know best.

Excited about writing a much more manageable piece, I opened my computer and typed the opening words of *Children on the Trail*.

About the Trail Guide

This guidebook covers the goals of the first few sections of the Trail, but it is much more than that. *Children on the Trail* has been written primarily as a guide for churches and parents who want to provide more effective spiritual nurture for children. It's about principles and it includes principles that can help churches create dynamic partnerships with parents.

As Reggie Joiner teaches, children and their families need both the yellow light (biblical teaching of the church) and the red heart (relational warmth of the home) to know and love God and become more like Jesus. In Joiner's book, the combination is represented by the colour orange.[7]

In *Children on the Trail*, churches and parents clasp hands across the Trail and work together on the same spiritual concepts and goals. And because spiritual formation for children happens best in the context of a vibrant faith community where people of every age enjoy caring relationships with one another, *Children on the Trail* is also about intergenerational ministry.

This book is first and foremost about principles. The intentional way in which we put these principles into practice will need to be constantly adapted to our ever-changing world. Many of the suggestions I make for the practical application of Trail principles are already outdated, but I offer them without apology. It is my prayer that even if certain practices are outdated, they will seed ideas for fresh and relevant ways to precipitate the spiritual formation of children in your moment of time.

Your moment already looks much different than mine. Before I finished writing this book, the world was in the throes of the COVID-19 pandemic. To keep the virus from spreading, physical gatherings of the church were either prohibited or diminished in size. Many churches continued their ministries, including children's ministries, online.

We wonder what the post-pandemic church will be like. But whether it's like the institutionalized church I have known, a hybrid of physical and virtual gatherings, a return to the New Testament house model, or something else, sound principles for effective children's ministry will adapt. Furthermore, these principles will work with either large groups of children or smaller ones of only two or three.

The book is also about intentionality. Producing effective spiritual formation in children requires us to be intentional in many

---

7 Joiner, *Think Orange*, 24.

About the Trail Guide

ways, but positive role-modelling and Bible stories are key. These keys are depicted by the two figures on the cover of this book: a caring older person walks the Trail with a child, their eyes on the Bible, God's written revelation of Himself, in which we also find Jesus, God's incarnational revelation of Himself.

Finally, *Children on the Trail* is about standing on the shoulders of the professors and authors who have taught me. It's about looking sideways at the great work my ministry colleagues and peers have done and are doing. It's about reaching deep into my own experience. And it's about putting it all between two covers for leaders and parents still to come.

Most of all, it's about trying to stay in the back seat on a tandem bike-like adventure with the Lord!

I am deeply grateful to The Crossing Church, formerly West End Baptist, which pioneered the Trail and gave me permission to share some of the resources we created. My thanks, too, to First Baptist in Moncton, New Brunswick and my colleagues there for their input, encouragement, and permission to share some of the Trail resources we developed.

My heartfelt thanks to my children's ministry colleagues who have been interested in this vision. I am especially grateful to Jody Linkletter (lecturer in New Generation Ministry at Acadia Divinity College), Tanya Yuen (Children and Family Ministries Associate for Canadian Baptists of Ontario and Quebec), and Dan Pyke (Director of Youth, and Family Ministries for Canadian Baptists of Atlantic Canada). Jody, Tanya, and Dan waded through my original manuscript, gave great suggestions for improving it, and then enriched the new version with several recommended resources.

My loving thanks, too, to Sarah Cogswell, soul friend and gifted children's pastor who made the journey through the project with me, editing it and offering many helpful suggestions.

Most of all, I want to thank my long-suffering and ever-loving partner in life and ministry, my husband the Rev. Dr. Gordon Sutherland. Gordon, an intentional parent himself, was the senior pastor who made space for the Trail at the West End Baptist Church. He has believed in this writing project from the beginning, ever encouraging me to keep on keeping on and always coming to my rescue when I couldn't get the computer to do what I wanted it to do.

This guidebook is not finished. We are surrounded by single parents, special needs children and their parents, grieving children and parents, and many other kinds of families who are not yet connected to a church. All of these parents need someone to write a chapter just for them. When I close my computer on *Children on the Trail*, will you open yours and write a sequel?

> *Let this be written for a future generation, that a people not yet created may praise the Lord.*
>
> —Psalm 102:18

Why Children and Children's Ministry Are Important

The phrase "They're small but not stupid" gets repeated in the Sutherland family a lot. It's been included in our family vocabulary ever since the day our teenage children, trying to help me with a Vacation Bible School lesson, cautioned me not to "dumb it down."

"Kids are small," they said, "but they're not stupid."

Sometimes churches make the mistake of thinking that because they are small, children are of little importance. In our adult-centric society, care and concern for adult issues can easily dominate the church.

But Jesus makes it clear that He wants His followers to serve those who tend to be overlooked: the powerless, the poor, the elderly, and the children (Mark 9:35–36). When you commit to working with children on the Trail, you may have to become an advocate for children's ministry. You may have to challenge other adults to free up ministry spaces, adjust church schedules, and expand church budgets for the sake of the children. You may have to urge others to get involved in children's ministry despite the sacrifices and energy it requires.

You may also have to persuade your lead pastor to champion children. With an already full to overflowing plate of responsibilities, lead pastors typically abandon children and children's ministry to auxiliary staff and/or volunteers. But lead pastors don't only have an important enabling influence on parents and others who work directly with children; they are also important role models for the children themselves.

Make an appointment to speak with your lead pastor about your vision for children on the Trail. Dream together about ways the vision can shape your church culture. Talk about the importance of children's ministry. Discuss these compelling principles:

- Jesus says that children are important.
- Children develop a worldview.
- The Gospel meets children's developmental needs.
- God uses children to do Kingdom work.
- God uses children to bring others to Himself.

1. Jesus says that children are important. Jesus teaches that children are exemplary citizens of heaven. In Mark 10:14–15, Jesus says,

> *Let the little children come to me, and do not hinder them, for the kingdom of God belongs to such as these. Truly I tell you, anyone who will not receive the kingdom of God like a little child will never enter it.*

There is undoubtedly much about little children that Jesus wants us to imitate: their beautiful innocence and disarming honesty, the way they are so quick to love and play, laugh and cry, and the fact that they are experts at forgiving and don't seem to know how to hold a grudge.

But the Bible consistently teaches that in order to be part of God's Kingdom, we need something else that is much more apparent in children than adults: a child's dependence on someone bigger and wiser and stronger than they are, and their unwavering trust in someone greater to protect them and provide what they need. The Bible calls this faith and consistently points out that no one can be part of God's Kingdom without it.

> *And without faith it is impossible to please God, because anyone who comes to him must believe that he exists and that he rewards those who earnestly seek him.*
> —Hebrews 11:6

> *For it is by grace you have been saved, through faith—and this is not from yourselves, it is the gift of God—not by works, so that no one can boast.*
> —Ephesians 2:8–9

> *Therefore, since we have been justified through faith, we have peace with God through our Lord Jesus Christ, through whom we have gained access by faith into this grace in which we now stand.*
> —Romans 5:1–2

> *I have been crucified with Christ and I no longer live, but Christ lives in me. The life I now live in the body, I live by faith in the Son of God, who loved me and gave himself for me.*
> —Galatians 2:20

> *The righteous will live by faith.*
> —Romans 1:17, Galatians 3:11
> (see also Hebrews 10: 38, Habakkuk 2:4)

Jesus teaches that children lead the way into God's Kingdom with their simple faith in Him and that the rest of us had better scramble to catch up!

We must also be very careful not to get in the way of children coming to Jesus. He said, *"Let the little children come to me, and do not hinder them"* (Matthew 19:14, Mark 10:14, Luke 18:16). These words of Jesus are recorded by three of the Gospel writers, so they must be important!

Jesus also gave a dire warning:

He called a little child to him, and placed the child among them. And he said: "Truly I tell you, unless you change and become like little children, you will never enter the kingdom of heaven. Therefore, whoever takes the lowly position of this child is the greatest in the kingdom of heaven. And whoever welcomes one such child in my name welcomes me.

"If anyone causes one of these little ones—those who believe in me—to stumble, it would be better for them to have a large millstone hung around their neck and to be drowned in the depths of the sea."

—Matthew 18:2–6

A dire warning indeed. Little children seem to arrive in the world with the internal knowledge that a watching, caring God exists. Woe on us for relegating them to the sidelines of the church when we should be keeping them front and centre to both lead them to Jesus *and* learn from their loving, faith-filled responses to Him.

2. Children develop a worldview. Children's ministry is also important because the things we experience and learn as children tend to shape the way we look at God, ourselves, and life itself for the rest of our lives.

Some sources credit the Jesuits and others, Aristotle, with having said, "Give me a child until he is seven and I will show you the man." What we learn in the first years of our lives is foundational and difficult to unlearn.

The way we see God and the world around us is called a worldview. We all have a worldview, no matter how confused or faulty it may be. Each person's worldview is shaped and formed by the worldview of people who influence them, by information they receive and how they process it, and by experiences they have and how they respond to them. A person's worldview begins to take shape the moment they enter the world.

It's very important that we give children the right worldview—that is, God's perspective—from the very beginning. As soon as children begin to interact with other caregivers, watch TV, hear stories, play with other children, and most certainly when they start school, they are introduced to other worldviews. The older children get, the more these other influences accumulate and the harder it can be to sort it all out.

Some people might say that giving a child a biblical worldview is brainwashing and that it's better to let children make up their own minds about "religion." But even when we give children a biblical worldview, they must make up their own minds about it; they still must choose to believe.

Although it has been popular for churches to skip past children's ministry and invest heavily in youth ministry, if we wait for a child to become a teenager before introducing them to a biblical worldview, God's perspective will face stiff competition from more popular notions in culture.

Please don't misunderstand me. Faced with growing independence and a lot of tough decisions to make, teenagers need lots of help grasping God's perspective on life and its issues. However, a life that begins in childhood with the right perspective on God and the world He has made is a life that begins with a definitive perspective that God can enlarge and strengthen over time.

3. The Gospel meets children's developmental needs.
Many sincere adult Christ-followers were first drawn to Him as

children. When children are helped to know God, they can meet Him in a relationship that matches and satisfies their developmental needs.

For example, research shows that a child's conscience usually forms between the ages of eight and eleven. Children this age who are troubled by guilt are particularly open to the good news about Jesus and God's forgiveness.

Children even younger, between five and eight, typically want to please those who have authority in their lives, whether it's parents, teachers, or God Himself.

4. God uses children to do Kingdom work. We engage children in ministry and service opportunities—not just to teach children to serve God by caring for others, but also so God can bless others through them.

Children on the Trail have raised money to buy goats for hungry families in the majority world. They have sold used books to buy supplies for pastors in Africa and India. They have baked cookies and exchanged them for donations to the local food bank; they have even taken donated money and shopped for the food bank themselves. They have visited seniors in care homes and taken thank-you treats to firefighters.

5. God uses children to bring others to Himself. Often less inhibited than adults, children are especially good at bringing their friends to church. God uses children to ignite faith in their parents, too. Many parents will be drawn to a church that cares about their children and about them as parents. Whole families can be reached through an effective children's ministry.

There is nothing small or insignificant about the spiritual formation of children. Children may be small, but in God's Kingdom they are of huge importance.

Children and Spiritual Formation

I like Robert Mulholland's succinct definition of spiritual formation: "a process of being formed in the image of Christ for the sake of others."[8] Students of this transformational process all agree that God, not us, does the work of transformation. He even gives us a longing for it. Our part is to follow our longing into a deepening relationship with God and, in the safety of that loving relationship, cooperate with God when He shows us things that need to change. The things that need to change will inevitably be related to our understanding of Him, our understanding of ourselves, our relationship with God, and our relationships with others.

How can we help children embark on a lifelong journey toward a deepening relationship and formative surrender to God? How can we help them long for it and start out in life equipped with all the right gear, unencumbered by anything that would weigh them down or hold them back?

There are a number of things we can do.

1. We can help them know that God is. We can point them to God's glory, displayed in creation (Psalm 19:1–4). We can show them God's goodness in people, all of whom have been made in the image of God (Genesis 1:27). We can open the Bible, God's written revelation of Himself, to them (Romans 10:17). We can show them Jesus, God in human form (I Corinthians 4:4, Colossians 1:15).

---

8 M. Robert Mulholland Jr., *Invitation to a Journey: A Road Map for Spiritual Formation* (Downers Grove, IL: InterVarsity Press, 1993), 16.

2. We can help them grasp the right concept of God. For a long time, my own image of God was comprised of a lot of disconnected pieces. I knew in my head that the Bible says "God is love" and that He had forgiven me because of my faith in Jesus, but I also knew that God is righteous and wants me to live without sin. Feeling that God must be constantly displeased with me made it hard for me to want to be with Him, or even to know how to be with Him!

Then I heard one of my professors say that the most important thing for any of us to know about God is His mercy. Because unless we grasp in our hearts that God is above all merciful, we won't want to be with Him.

The Bible is clear that the single most all-encompassing aspect of God's nature is love (1 John 4:16). God's love is displayed in His mercy (Psalm 25:6, Isaiah 63:9, Ephesians 2:4). Full of mercy, God is always for us (John 3:17). Full of mercy, God never stops loving us; He does so unfailingly and unflinchingly, accepting us warts and all. Full of mercy, God is always willing to forgive us.

3. We can give our children a biblical worldview. By this, I mean that we can help them see the world, themselves, and other people the way God sees them. We can help them see with God's perspective what is good and not good.

This is critical in the process of spiritual formation. Becoming more like Christ involves recognizing what is not like Christ, yielding those things to God, and allowing God to fill up the newly vacated spaces within us with Himself.

4. We can help our children live in a posture of openness to God and complete dependence on Him. Not only can we intentionally teach and encourage our children to trust God with their needs, we can show them what a God-dependent life looks like. We can let our children see us spend regular time alone with God, bring our needs to God, and thank God for meeting our needs.

Parents and other significant adults in a child's life do all this by walking with a child through life, nurturing a close relationship with them and discovering God's thoughts with them. We read Bible stories with children and marvel over God out loud with them. We introduce faith and prayer to children as a natural way of life. We lean into God so He can make us the role models children need us to be, people who are loving God more deeply, following Him more nearly, and depending on Him more completely. And we help children become part of a faith community where they can experience corporate worship and service and engage with other role models and spiritual friends.

Will we, or even can we, provide these foundational pieces flawlessly? Of course not. When we tell children a Bible story, we will wish we had talked more effectively with the children about it. We won't always be the Christ-like example our children need to see, and neither can we always be part of a faith community that is consistently Christ-like. Faith communities are made up of people who, despite their faith, are only human. We are all still on the same spiritual growth journey we want our children to make.

Even though there will be wrong notes, even though we won't always choose to practice and sometimes not show up for performances, if the overall tone of our faith and obedience is infused with our love for God, we can trust Him to fill in the gaps and override our mistakes. He will work in and through the composition of all that we invest in our children. He is on the journey with them, and He is the One who will help them become all that He wants them to be. Our biggest responsibility is to keep our eyes on God the Conductor, not on ourselves.

Sometimes parents do their intentional best and their children still make heart-breaking choices. We cannot control our children. All we can do is offer God our intentional best, continue to trust

His grace for our children, and love both Him and our children no matter what.

We are only ever responsible for the choices we make. When we make wrong choices, the right choice is to confess the wrong we have done to God and our children and trust God, who is rich in mercy, to bring good even out of our mistakes.

Above all, we must remember that it is never too late for us or our children to experience God's grace and mercy. Remembering this, we continue to pray.

Spiritual formation is hard to measure. We can't track a child's spiritual growth with pencil marks on the wall. There aren't even structured tests for spiritual formation like the ones kids take to measure their progress at school. Nevertheless, God's work in a person's life is more real than what we perceive with our senses. Ask God to help you see Him at work in your child's life. Be encouraged when your child's thoughts, attitudes, and choices show that they are internalizing the spiritual concepts of the Trail.

As we grow older, we recognize the value of spiritual disciplines on our journey toward God. He often uses the practice of spiritual disciplines, however imperfect the practicing of them may be, to create spaces where He can touch our lives with His transforming grace. Interacting with significant role models, reflecting on stories from the Bible, and engaging in a faith community are spiritual disciplines that create space for God to work in a child's life.

So let's help children experience God's accepting, loving **Welcome**. Let's help them be full of **Wonder** over who God is. Let's help them constantly **Discover** more of God and His marvellous ways. And let's help **Launch** children into other spiritual disciplines so they can continue their journey toward God and Christlikeness.

Let's walk with children on this spiritual journey we call the Trail.

Welcome

Trail Section One: *Birth to Age Two*

In our family, we have home movies on a DVD that we watch almost every Christmas. The DVD shows that at little more than one year old, our daughter heard me say "Wave to Daddy" and responded by raising her hand and making fist pumps. It also shows her, at the same age, standing on her chair and then plopping onto her bottom when I looked at her and said, "Sit down, please."

Somehow, while we were busy feeding her, burping her, bathing her, changing her, and cuddling her, our tiny daughter watched our faces, listened to the tone of our voices, and even began to recognize words.

I'm glad we've had this DVD, but I wish I could go back, move more slowly, and watch the miracle unfold in real time.

About the Name

THE FIRST SECTION OF THE TRAIL IS CALLED WELCOME. THIS MINISTRY for babies and toddlers is designed to help the church celebrate with parents as they welcome a new child into their family. It is also designed to give little ones positive first impressions of the church and a warm welcome into the church family.

Some might argue that these littlest ones don't need the same kind of ministry investment that older children do, but Jesus took these smallest ones into His loving arms. Their ability to absorb and learn spiritually is truly amazing!

Although this section of the Trail is officially called Welcome, we began to call it the Welcome Circle when we spoke of it at First

Baptist in Moncton—to avoid it becoming confused with terms used by our hospitality ministry.

A Unique Welcome

Because the Welcome Circle is intended to serve parents as well as their young children, it should be fully staffed through the duration of each worship gathering even if no children arrive when it first opens. Sometimes parents like to keep their children with them for a while.

This is especially true if you have provided a "baby corner" in the back of your worship space. A baby corner is an inviting area where parents and grandparents can sit and rock infants during adult worship. But even parents who want to keep their infants with them are usually glad to bring them to the Welcome Circle when they become active toddlers!

Operating a Welcome Circle from the mentality that you're there to serve parents means that staff are sometimes on duty with no children in the room. When this happens, encourage volunteers to grab a coffee and visit with each other, as long as the coffee disappears when the first child arrives! Because of the Welcome Circle's unique dynamics, recruiting volunteers for the same Sunday each month, on a monthly rotation, seems to work well.

About Welcome Children

Cognitively. Babies and toddlers are nonverbal, or barely verbal, but they are smart and learn rapidly. Research indicates that a baby's brain doubles in size the first year.

Dr. Nancy Lass has written that children are most receptive to learning in the first four years of their lives.[9] How important is it, then, to include an introduction to Jesus in this foundational learning!

Babies and toddlers learn through all five senses. They learn as they move, touch, taste, listen, and watch. They also learn by imitating what they have seen or heard. Researchers tell us that babies can hear voices while they are still in the womb. After they are born, they love to watch your face and listen as you talk. At two weeks old, a baby is more interested in a human face than anything else—and by the time they are two months old, they can match a face with a voice.[10]

So make eye contact with babies when you talk to them. Have fun varying your voice, making animal sounds, and repeating the sounds they make. A baby cooing is a baby learning to talk!

Physically. Babies and toddlers grow so fast that they change a little every day. Because they grow so fast, they thrive on movement. Infants need time and space to kick their feet and wave their arms. Rolling over leads to crawling, and crawling to walking, until as toddlers they seem to be always on the go.

Emotionally. These littlest ones are emotionally perceptive and positively affected by happy, loving impressions created by people in their environment. Babies need to be lovingly touched and held to feel secure and emotionally well.

Babies can't meet their own needs, so they cry to make their needs known. Toddlers, who are just beginning to emerge from absolute dependence on others, are apt to swing from brief bouts of independence to wanting lots of hugs and cuddles. It is common

---

9 Shirley Morgenthaler, *Right from the Start: A Parent's Guide to the Young Child's Faith Development* (St. Louis, MO: Concordia Publishing, 2001). Foreword by Dr. Nancy Lass.
10 Ibid., 49.

for babies and toddlers to experience separation anxiety at eight months, twelve months, and then again between eighteen months to three years.

Socially. Toddlers tend to play on their own, but it's still good for them to be with other children. They learn by watching others, including other children.

Imagine a young family pulling into the church parking lot on Sunday morning, a dad and mom with a two-year-old and a five-month-old baby. They're running late because the two-year-old accidently spilled his morning cereal all over himself and had to be cleaned up before they could leave the house. The baby hasn't been sleeping through the night, so the parents are already tired and draggy.

Imagine the dad uttering a heartfelt "Thank You, Lord" as he parks in one of the spaces reserved for families with young children. It's near the door, next to the parking spots reserved for seniors.

When they enter the church foyer, each parent loaded down with a child and all the child's paraphernalia, an older woman's face lights up. She hurries toward them with outstretched arms. The young mom feels herself begin to relax for the first time that morning.

The older woman cuddles the baby while the parents get the two-year-old settled and playing happily in the Welcome Circle.

The baby falls asleep, so the older woman sits and holds her during the worship service. The young mom sinks into the seat beside her. The dad hands the young mom a cup of coffee and she begins to breathe more slowly, drawing in the very presence of God and releasing her weariness and stress to Him.

In the sacred stillness, she hears the Lord say, His Spirit to her spirit, "You are doing one of the most important jobs in the world. I love you and I will help you." *The young mom's heart overflows with gratitude and worship.*

Welcome Trail Goals

- God Made Me
- Jesus Loves Me
- Church Is a Happy Place to Be
- Church Is a Family for My Family

God made me. Talk with the child about things God has made. Say, "God made apples. Thank You, God, for apples!" Help children use as many of their five senses as possible to explore different things God has made.

Show them pictures—whether on the wall or in storybooks—of animals, people, and other things God has created. Use simple language. For example, "God made puppies. I love puppies. Puppies say 'bow-wow!' Thank You, God, for puppies." Or use their name: "God made *(child's name)*. God loves *(child's name)*. Thank You, God, for *(child's name)*."

Play simple games that engage their eyes, hands, ears, and feet. For example, play Peek-a-boo and say, "God made eyes so we can see! God made you and God made me!" Then ring a bell and say, "I can hear the bell. God made ears so we can hear. Thank You, God, for ears!"

Point out colours God has made. Say, "The tree is green. God made trees. God made green. Thank You, God, for trees and green."

Learn a simple God-made-me rhyme and have fun repeating it to a child while you touch their fingers, toes, etc. Say, "God made my fingers. God made my toes. God made my brown eyes. God made my nose."

Jesus loves me. Pray before you go to work in the Welcome Circle and while you're there. Ask God to let His love flow through you to each child.

Whenever you tell the child "God made you," add the truth: "And He loves you."

Sing simple songs, like "Jesus Loves Me," "Jesus Loves the Little Children," and "Jesus Loves the Little Ones Like Me, Me, Me."

Sing praise songs and hymns about Jesus, especially when you're trying to soothe a distraught or tired child.

Pray for the child while they're sleeping and when you hold them in your arms. Thank God for them. Ask God to give the child faith in Him.

Church is a happy place to be. Do all you can to help each child experience church as a loving, safe, and happy place. Children learn the value of faith by absorbing the consistent attitudes of the community around them. We personalize God's love for children!

Advocate for the needs and best interests of these littlest ones and their families.

Church is a family for my family. Nurture caring relationships with parents. Take their concerns and suggestions seriously. Comply with their concerns and suggestions whenever their ideas don't compromise policies or practices put in place for the safety and best interests of all children and families.

Help parents and the church welcome new babies and celebrate their arrival with Welcome Circle baby showers. Baby showers can be hosted by the Welcome Circle ministry team or by specially appointed volunteers. The whole church can be invited to baby showers. Including everyone turns a baby shower into an intergenerational event.

Conduct Ceremonies of Promise and Blessing with parents.[11] Include a preparation session that helps parents understand the commitment they're making and explains sound principles for nurturing faith at home.[12]

Recruit someone on your Welcome Circle ministry team to record the birthdates of all the little ones in the Welcome ministry. Have them mail a card to each child on their first and second birthdays.

Encourage parents to nurture their own personal relationship with God. Continue to offer spiritual formation opportunities for adults and specific help for parents. Encourage parents to become engaged in other ministries, friendship opportunities, and intergenerational events the church provides.

Welcome Curriculum

We are so accustomed to simply providing childcare for babies and toddlers that it may be easy to overlook the importance of intentional teaching in the Welcome Circle.

But one mom said, "If my baby isn't going to learn about Jesus in the church nursery, I would rather care for her myself in the sanctuary." Perhaps we simply need help to know how to make the most of this opportunity.

Good curricula for the Welcome Circle will help us achieve the Welcome Trail goals. It will supply simple songs, rhymes, and perhaps even visuals. It will also suggest plenty of ways in which we can intentionally and lovingly talk with children about God while we play with them. For example:

---

11 See Appendix 1: Ceremony of Promise and Blessing.
12 See Appendix 2: Godly Parenting.

- Pretend you cannot see the toddler. Say: "Where is *(child's name)*? I can't find her!"
- Pretend to look all around for the child. Talk about the places you look. Say: "She's not under the table. Where is she? She's not playing with the blocks. Where is she?"
- Then look directly at the child. Say: "Oh, there she is! I'm so glad I found *(child's name)*. I love her and Jesus loves her!"

The Welcome Circle Space

One of the most appealing aspects of the Welcome Circle space for parents and grandparents will be its physical proximity to the space where they worship. Ideally, the Welcome Circle should be on the same level as the adult worship centre. It's hard for parents and grandparents to carry babies and toddlers up and down stairs with a diaper bag slung over their shoulder and sometimes another young child in tow.

Even more critically, today's parents are more concerned about their child's safety than anything else. Knowing their child is on a different level and/or far away in the building can make parents anxious and reluctant to use the Welcome Circle, or even reluctant to come to church at all.

Another important requirement for the Welcome Circle is that it be kept clean and as safe as possible. Provide sanitizing resources such as disinfectant liquid or spray for wiping the surfaces on change tables, cribs, and rocking chairs; disinfectant wipes for cleaning toys; alcoholic hand wash for volunteers; and if possible a sink with warm water and soap.

Keep the floor as clear as possible. Set baskets of toys against the walls. Discard any toys and objects that could harm a child, such as items with sharp or metallic surfaces. These include jewellery, cords, batteries, latex balloons, tippy ride-on toys, large toy boxes or bins with covers, and toys small enough or with parts small enough to be a choking hazard (small cars, Lego, button eyes, etc.). Discard plush toys for sanitary reasons and include soft rubber toys instead.

Include only soft covered or small board books for babies and toddlers with few words and large, simple pictures. These should be books that show things God has made or communicate "Jesus loves me" messages. Remember that babies see in black and white before they perceive the primary colours.

Remove toys that have been in a child's mouth, placing them in a mesh bag and taking them home to be washed in a dishwasher or with hot soapy water. Or use a sanitizing spray and leave them in a bin to air-dry.

Ask adults to remove their shoes before entering the room. Provide knitted slippers for volunteers. Removing shoes not only helps keep the room clean, it also helps prevent injury. If an adult accidentally steps on little fingers, for example, soft slippers will do less danger than heavier, harder shoes! Toddlers who are walking should also have their shoes replaced with grip sole socks. Provide a basket or laundry bin for used slippers and socks and take these home regularly to be laundered and returned.

It is also important to establish rules about who is and isn't allowed in the Welcome Circle. Typically, only the children themselves, the volunteers on duty, and parents invited in by volunteers to help calm a child should be allowed in the room. Explain to older children who might want to come in to play, as well as to other adult visitors, that the room must be kept sanitized for the little ones and their caregivers.

Use a Dutch door, one that is cut into a top and bottom half, for the Welcome Circle. Train volunteers to keep the bottom half of the door closed while they're caring for children in the room and only close and bolt the top half when the room isn't being used and/or if the whole door must be closed and bolted for safety reasons. Closing the lower part of the door keeps out people who shouldn't be in the nursery. Parents can hand their children over the door to a volunteer on the other side. Keeping the top part of the door open allows it to serve as a window into the room and makes the Welcome Circle compliant with recommended child protection policies.[13]

Soften the floor with bright rubber foam mats. These come in varying sizes and can be fitted together like pieces of a puzzle. They are perfect for crawling, sitting on the floor to play, and cushioning falls! They also help to brighten the room.

The room can be painted a soft white or pastel shade. Decorate with creation themes (for example, a rainbow, farm animals, etc.) rather than popular cartoon characters. Attach bright, simple pictures and posters to the walls at the level of a child's eyes when they're being carried around the room. These pictures and posters should show animals, people, colours, and other things God has made. Post pictures of children from different racial/cultural backgrounds.

Design and provide a Welcome Circle brochure that introduces parents to the Welcome Circle and outlines the policies. Parents typically want to know the answers to several key questions: "Who will care for my baby? How safe and clean is this space? How will being here help my baby? What do I need to know about how the Welcome Circle works?"

---

13 See Appendix 3: Sample Child Protection Policy.

Wonder

Trail Section Two: *Ages Three to Four*

One Christmas Eve, my husband and I dressed our young children in bathrobes, draped dish towels over their heads, and had them playact the Christmas story.

It was well past bedtime when the priceless performance neared its end. Since I was the narrator, I decided to wrap things up quickly.

"After the wise men came," I said, tipping each stuffed toy magi into a bow as they presented their gifts to the baby Jesus, "Mary and Joseph took the baby Jesus and went home."

"No, Mommy," said our three-year-old son, standing so abruptly and with such consternation that his oversized, worn-backwards bathrobe almost slid off. "They went to Egypt."

Three years old and following Jesus!

About the Name

THE SECOND SECTION OF THE TRAIL IS CALLED WONDER. THIS MINISTRY, for preschool children, is designed to celebrate the sense of wonder little ones have at this age as they begin to interact with the world God made.

The word "wonder" also refers to the fresh openness young children have for God Himself. It's as though they've just been with Him and have landed on earth with the simple knowledge that God is and that God is good!

This is the pure, uncluttered faith of a child that Jesus says we all must have. It shows up best in preschool children because they aren't yet hindered by self-consciousness and all the worldly perspectives and attitudes we tend to collect as we age.

Wonder is all about capitalizing on a young child's sense of spiritual wonder and strengthening it while we can!

About Wonder Children

Even though each Wonder child is a unique individual and needs to be known for who they are, there are some cognitive, physical, emotional, and social characteristics common to children this age.

Cognitively. Children between the ages of three and four are short... and they have short attention spans! There are always exceptions, of course—and the more interactive the story presentation, the longer they will listen—but the general rule is to measure a preschool child's attention span by their age. Wonder children can only listen well for three or four minutes at a time.

Wonder children learn by engaging all their senses. It's very important for them to be able to touch and explore things with their hands. Instead of saying "Don't touch!" provide lots of objects they can hold and manipulate. As writer GiGi Schweikert has said, "Let them take a few minutes to explore the way the cover fits over the felt tip of a marker before they use the marker!"[14]

Adults commonly make the mistake of talking too much when working with preschool children. Ask, "What do you think?" Then listen to the child as if they were the only person in the room.

Let preschool children talk, even if it's nonsense. As these little ones hear and use words they don't yet understand, they are learning to express themselves and building a vocabulary. Sprinkle your teaching with repetitive words, rhyming words, and silly words they can use.

---

14 GiGi Schweikert, "3–5 Age Level Insights," *Children's Ministry Magazine*, July-August 2011.

Three- and four-year-old children are very curious. They learn by asking questions. Expect plenty of "why" questions. We want to encourage children to keep on asking questions as they grow up, so patiently respond to their "why" questions with simple answers.

Preschool children have a tremendous capacity for learning. They not only can learn; they want to learn!

But even though learning explodes in the preschool years, children this age can only do one thing at a time and they aren't yet able to connect ideas. Limit your instructions to just one or two ideas at a time. Present them in simple, separate sentences instead of combining thoughts.

For example, say, "Peter was Jesus's helper. John was Jesus's helper" rather than "Peter and John were both Jesus's helpers." Realize that they can't yet connect ideas, which may make it hard for them to remember last week's story.

Children this age also think literally. This means they can't think beyond the symbol to grasp the concept behind it. For example, for decades we have taught children to sing "This Little Light of Mine," but preschool children can't grasp the symbolic significance of the word "light." The song probably makes them think of holding an actual candle or flashlight in their hand. Also, because these little ones take everything literally, be careful not to tease them.

Preschool children have big, lively imaginations! They love to play, and they learn while playing, so have fun playing and pretending with them. Keep in mind that fantasy and reality are still intertwined for them. Because this is so, expect them to exaggerate, have imaginary friends, and believe everything they're told.

Physically. These children grow rapidly! They need to move around a lot to give their big motor skills a chance to develop. Have them sit on the floor rather than on chairs and give them plenty of opportunities to jump, dance, and march. Because they're growing so fast, they tire easily. Balance active time with rest.

Preschool children are developing their small motor skills, too. Let them use crayons and scissors. Be careful not to do everything for them, but because preschoolers are easily frustrated when things don't go their way, be prepared to step in and help.

Surprisingly enough, colouring a picture may not be an ideal activity for a preschool child. Because their small motor skills are still developing, it's hard for them to stay within the lines. Instead of giving them pictures to colour, consider giving them crayons and blank paper so they can create their own "pictures."

Remember that even though these little ones love to talk, their vocal cords are still developing. That means it's hard for them to carry a tune. Sing with them, but expect it to be a joyful noise! Also, expect children this age to be noisy and boisterous. Patiently encourage them to use their indoor voices.

Wonder children are susceptible to colds and are apt to either miss time because they're not feeling well or show up with a runny nose!

Emotionally. Three- and four-year-old children have intense emotions. They can go from tears to laughter, and vice versa, in a matter of seconds. As Gigi Scweikert says, their intense emotions can "impact their motivation, attentiveness, and sense of self-worth. Let them explain themselves when they show intense emotion and don't discount how they feel."[15]

Help children name their feelings. If a child is frustrated because she can't find her shoes, say, "You're feeling frustrated because you can't find your shoes." Another way to help children learn to use words for their feelings is to look at pictures of people in storybooks and name the feeling expressed on each character's face.

---

15 Ibid.

Wonder children are comforted by routine and repetition. In fact, an effective Wonder lesson plan provides a calming routine sprinkled with just a dose of adventure and novelty.

A helpful rule of thumb is to spend eighty percent of Wonder time in a consistent way. For example, start with an introduction to the main Bible point, then tell the Bible story and talk about it. This can be followed by an activity that connects the main point to their lives. The remaining twenty percent of the time can be a surprise—for example, a special visitor or fun snack.

Because these little ones are often afraid of new places, experiences, and people, expect them to feel shy when anything changes. Give them time and space to adjust. Encourage them with gentle reassurances. Don't be surprised if they cleave to their parents. Separation anxiety sometimes returns after a two-year-old has fought for their independence. Assure the child that their parents will be back soon and distract them with a new toy, book, or activity.

Another emotion prevalent among three- and four-year-old children is jealousy, especially when it comes to adult attention. Children this age really want adults to notice them, so do your best to give generous and equal attention to all of them.

Socially. Preschool children think adults are wonderful and automatically imitate them, even their attitudes and attributes! Use the children's names and let them use yours.

Kneel to talk with them, and humble yourself to enter their world. For example, play and colour with them instead of just watching them. Affirm and encourage them whenever you can. They love to help, so let them help. They trust adults; if you say you're going to do something, see that you do it!

Preschool children tend to invade each other's space when they play and copycat each other. They can't be expected to be unselfish yet, but they can learn to be more thoughtful of others. They have trouble taking turns and sharing and will need coaching, but fairness is very important to them, so expect to hear the expression "No fair" a lot! They may playact bullying, but there's no need to interfere unless they are really bullying one another.

Wonder children can understand that wrong behaviours have consequences. They will test the rules, so make sure these are simple and easy to enforce. Because young children have little concept of time, it's important to enforce the consequences immediately.

Imagine a three- or four-year- old who talks to Jesus as freely and candidly as he talks to his very best friend. This little one knows that Jesus is right beside him because he sees Jesus with the eyes of his heart. He knows that Jesus speaks to him through God's special book, the Bible. He loves and respects the Bible and longs for the day when he can read it for himself. He knows the first story in the Bible tells about how God made the world and every pond and animal and person in it. And when this Little One encounters both delightful and rocky patches on his journey through life, he'll still be talking to Jesus and opening God's Word to hear Jesus speak to him because he has found that the Jesus he learned to love as a child is still his Best Friend.

Wonder Trail Goals

- God Made Everything
- Jesus Is My Best Friend
- I Can Talk to Jesus Anywhere, Anytime, About Anything
- The Bible Is God's Special Book

Remember that Trail goals are designed to be cumulative. Continue to include Welcome Circle goals and concepts in all your Wonder teaching.

God made everything. Start your Wonder curriculum with Bible stories about creation. Then, even after you've moved on to other stories, continue to convey this truth with your own natural acknowledgement of God as Creator.

For example, when you look at pictures of birds, say, "Isn't it wonderful that God made birds?" Add the word "wonder" to your comment: "I wonder how God made birds so they can fly!" Take time to help the children see that God gave birds different colours; He also made some, like the hummingbird, very small while others, like the eagle, are very big. Make simple thank-you prayers for things God made a regular part of your vocabulary. For example, "Thank You, God, for making birds that fly."

Include songs and rhymes about God's creation in your ongoing lesson plans.

Don't feel that you have to correct a child's theology if they hold up a manufactured item such as a pencil and say, "God made pencils." A child's theology grows as the child grows.

But be prepared to give a child an honest answer if they ask a direct question like, "Did God make pencils?" The simplest answer is "God helps people make things like pencils."

One day my sister overheard a conversation between my three- and five-year-old nieces. While pulling their boots on, the three-year-old asked the five-year-old, "God made your boots?"

"No," said the five-year-old. "But God made the shoemaker who made my boots."

After a thoughtful moment, the three-year-old said, "I like God."

And the five-year-old agreed: "Yeah, I like God, too."

Jesus is my best friend. Include Bible stories of Jesus and His helping, saving love in your Wonder curriculum. For example, tell a story about Jesus being a best friend to the children who were brought to Him, or about Jesus being a best friend to Zacchaeus.

Help the children see Jesus in the Scriptures as clearly and personally as if they had stepped into the Bible story themselves. Focus on His love that extends beyond the Bible story to each one of the children and to you. Our love for Him, ourselves, and others begins by thrilling to God's love for us.

Let your personal love and adoration of Jesus shine through in that all you do and say. Teach the children to turn to Jesus for help with their Wonder-sized challenges. Remind the children to thank Jesus for all the help He gives them.

I can talk to Jesus anywhere, anytime, about anything. Model this for the children. Pepper your conversations with short prayers about little things and big things. Remind the children that Jesus is always with us and hears us no matter where we are. He even hears the prayers we whisper and the prayers we pray quietly in our hearts!

Explain that we often close our eyes when we talk to Jesus because that helps us think about Him instead of things we see around us... but we can talk to Jesus with our eyes open, too!

Although you should pray spontaneously with the children, also include more formal prayer times. Routinely ask the children to sit quietly with their heads bowed to show respect for Jesus, folding their hands to keep them out of trouble and closing their eyes so they can think about Jesus. Then lead them in short sentence prayers that they can repeat line by line after you, either out loud or in their hearts.

The Bible is God's special book. Much of what shapes a child's thoughts and attitudes are the thoughts and attitudes they absorb from significant adults in their lives. If you love the Bible and display your respect and gratitude for it, the children around you will, too. Be sure to demonstrate the way you value the Bible by bringing it out and showing it to the children every time you're ready to tell them a story from it.

Before you tell a Bible story, take a few minutes to show the children the same story in a children's Bible. Along with teaching the children that the Bible is God's special book, this simple practice shows the children that the stories you tell aren't make-believe. It also encourages the child to find the story you have told them in their own Bible when they go home.

Wonder Curriculum

Each Bible lesson should present one main truth, and this single truth should be repeated frequently throughout the lesson in different ways. Young children learn through repetition. Giving them the opportunity to interact with the same idea in a variety of ways adds adventure to learning. Look for an assortment of learning activities in each lesson, activities that maximize learning by engaging a young child's five senses.

Choose a curriculum that presents creation stories from the Old Testament and stories of Jesus's birth, life, death, and resurrection from the New Testament. These Bible stories should be written in a short, simple style and enhanced with large, brightly coloured visuals. Plan to make Bible stories even more interesting by:

- displaying additional visuals such as objects or costumes from biblical times.
- matching your facial expression to what a character is feeling. Because young children have strong emotional responses, downplay the more traumatic parts

of Bible stories, such as the Egyptians falling into the sea, Jesus suffering on the cross, etc.
- talking slower or faster to make parts of the story more dramatic.
- whispering to build suspense, shouting when a character shouts, and gesturing with your hands.
- ending the story with a summary of the lesson's main biblical truth and stopping there! Wonder stories need to be short and sweet.

Wonder curricula sometimes will include music that supports the main truth. Because three- and four-year-olds are instinctively drawn to repetition, they will enjoy singing the same songs again and again. These can be songs with plenty of movement, songs that can be enjoyed with rhythm instruments, or songs that can be sung with sign language and other hand motions.

Check to see if the curriculum includes puppet scripts. Young children will soon lose interest in a conversation between two adults, but they are easily mesmerized by a talking puppet! If you invest in a Wonder puppet, give it a name, personality, and playful sense of humour. You don't have to be a talented puppeteer to use a Wonder puppet. Simply enjoy the puppet as much as the children do!

No matter how wonderful a published curriculum may be, it's only intended to be a library of ideas for teachers to use. Effective teachers are artists. They may use materials others have provided, but they design and create unique learning experiences for the children entrusted to their care.

Curriculum writers bring their own theological and pedagogical expertise to the material they produce, but the teachers who work with these materials are experts when it comes to knowing Trail goals, the children in their group, and the limitations of their teaching space and equipment. Wonderful curricula and wonderful teachers trained in the artistic use of curricula are a winning combination!

The Wonder Space

In our churches, we called the room we used Wonder World and decorated it with a creation theme. Paint the room a soft shade and then post large tree, pond, and/or animal cutouts on the walls. Or have someone with artistic ability paint a creation/animal kingdom mural. Use primary colours. Each one of these primary colours is a wonderful gift from God and an integral part of His creation: blue sky, green grass, red roses, etc.

Your Wonder World should include a storytelling circle on the floor. Use a large rug or foam mats that come in bright, primary colours and fit together like a jigsaw puzzle. Sometimes retailers will give you carpet samples. Let each child choose their own spot on the foam mat or their own carpet piece so they know exactly where to land when sent back to their place in the circle.

Ideally, a Wonder World also includes at least one child-sized table and chair set (for snacks and/or crafts), an open space for moving, and as many of the following play centres as possible:

- block centre.
- housekeeping centre.
- book centre.
- handwork centre (for playdough, puzzles, drawing, etc.).
- alternating centre. This can be a music centre one day and a nature centre another. Or it could be a low-to-the ground bulletin board.

Playtime is a very important part of a Wonder lesson. Through play, young children learn by talking and getting along with others. They also develop better hand-eye coordination, remember what they have experienced, assimilate new ideas, and absorb new values. So provide space and time to play and give each child the freedom to choose the play activity that interests them most.

Design your Wonder World with the children in mind. Crawl around the room on your hands and knees to see the room from a child's perspective. It's frustrating not to be able to see over or around adult furniture. Keep the room clean, neat, uncluttered, and free of anything that could be a danger to them.

Discover

Trail Section Three: *Ages Five to Eight*

One afternoon a week, I showed up at our local community centre to help the kids with their homework.

One day I helped a seven-year-old boy. He and I hit it off and became regulars. I would wait for him to come from school, and he would come into the centre looking for me. But we spent less than an hour together each week and it seemed to my cluttered adult mind that our relationship must surely be only on the periphery of his life.

Imagine my surprise when years later, after I had moved away and he had grown into a thoughtful teenager, the director at the centre told me that he often asked about me and expressed concern for my well-being.

I've since realized that everything is big to a child, including and perhaps especially a caring relationship with an adult, no matter how limited it is.

About the Name

The third section of the Trail is called Discover. What an appropriate name for a group of children who are learning to read and write, memorize, problem-solve, create, and move here, there, and everywhere! They turn everything into an adventure as they discover life itself. They are geared to explore and experience as they leave the greater protection of their preschool years and take their first steps into growing autonomy.

God's intended support for them in the early years of this transition are warm, caring relationships with adults who guide and encourage them, show them how to do life well, and help them centre themselves in God. The best Discover teachers refrain from telling children what they need to know. Instead they create endless opportunities for children to discover it on their own! These wise teachers realize that we are all far more apt to absorb truth when we discover it for ourselves.

About Discover Children

Even though each Discover child is unique, with emerging differences in personalities and learning styles, children this age share some general characteristics. Understanding who Discover children typically are cognitively, physically, emotionally, and socially helps us lay a good foundation for their spiritual learning experiences.

Cognitively. Because children change significantly from one year to the next in their Discover years, a five-year-old may be quite different from a six-, seven-, or eight-year-old. A five-year-old still learns mostly by doing. However, although we still learn best when all our physical senses are engaged, six- and seven-year-old children begin to be auditory learners—that is, they learn a lot simply by listening. They also learn a lot by putting their thoughts into their own words. Yes, that's right. They learn by talking!

Five- and six-year-olds may still have trouble sorting fantasy from reality. But kids who are seven and eight will be more apt to recognize the difference between true stories and fiction. They will enjoy both.

Because the youngest Discover children still tend to take things literally, avoid symbolic words and phrases. Use simple, clear words that mean what they say and say what they mean.

For example, when a child hears phrases like "Ask Jesus to come into your heart," they may picture Jesus stepping into a Valentine's Day heart! Use phrases like "Trust Jesus to be your Saviour" and "Love and obey Jesus" instead.

Remember, though, that seven-year-olds are beginning to think logically. They love collecting and sorting things! They also love facts, riddles, and corny jokes. Wrap your teaching in a playful attitude. Karl Bastian, the founder of Kidology.org, recommends putting on a silly hat, saying things incorrectly, and making silly mistakes like pretending to trip when you walk on stage.[16]

Seven- and eight-year-olds can stay focused for fifteen to twenty minutes if they're engaged in the learning experience. Younger Discover children will have shorter attention spans. We will need to adjust our expectations for these younger children and either shorten learning experiences for their sake or have other activities ready for them when they lose interest in an experience that holds the attention of the older children.

Young Discover children still do best with one idea at a time. They tend to think of things in parts instead of a whole. For example, they can understand that Jesus is God's Son, but probably not that Jesus is also God. They also have trouble grasping the concept of time and think and live in the present. They may need help and encouragement to move from one step of a project to the next.

Six- and seven-year-olds are beginning to read and are quick to memorize short sentences, especially if they can see them in print. The fact that they're starting to read is exciting, and of course we will want to cheer them on, but it's best not to ask beginners to read in front of other children. Reading out loud can be hard and stressful for them, and because they read slowly the other children will quickly become bored.

As they take their first steps into a lifetime of learning, six- and seven-year-olds want to get things right. They tend to be perfectionists, so it takes them a long time to do anything. Be careful not to criticize. Encourage them to do their best and praise them

---

16 Karl Bastian, "Make 'em Laugh," *Children's Ministry Magazine*, January-February 2017.

for their efforts, not their accomplishments. Accept the fact that you'll be sending home lots of unfinished projects!

The cognitive differences between the youngest and oldest children in Discover make teaching this group a challenge. The more children at each specific age, the bigger the challenge! Some churches have a Discover 1 group for children between the ages of five and six, and a Discover 2 group for children between the ages of seven and eight.

Physically. Discover kids seem to be in perpetual motion. They're physically active because their large muscles are constantly growing and developing.

Understand that anything is more exciting for them than sitting still. So let them stand and move about to do crafts and other activities. Let them sprawl on the floor when they listen to a story. Better yet, let them playact the story!

Give Discover kids time and space to run and jump, but plan games that are cooperative rather than competitive. Every Discover kid wants to be first. It's distressing for them when there can be only one winner and it's not them! Comfort them with phrases like "We feel disappointed when we don't win, but you played very well! Perhaps you'll win next time."

Discover kids are ready for interesting crafts, but their small motor skills are still developing. The youngest children may still have some hand-eye coordination challenges, so don't expect them to cut with scissors precisely or colour inside the lines. Praise their efforts!

Emotionally. Discover kids typically feel shy and anxious about new experiences. It's natural for Discover kids to have fears as the world begins to open to them. They may want to talk about ghosts, bullies, pandemics, earthquakes, floods, and even death if a pet or someone they love has recently died.

Don't ignore or sidestep their comments. Acknowledge their feelings. For example, say things like "It's scary when there's a pandemic" or "It's sad when someone dies." Ask gentle questions: "What do you think is the scariest part? What is the saddest part? How can God help us?" Expect them to ask "why" questions. Be honest about not knowing "why." It's okay for children to know that adults don't have all the answers. Only God does.[17]

When you tell Bible stories, remember that children this age are especially sensitive to sadness. If a story seems sad or scary, reassure them that they can trust God to help with things that are sad or scary. They have a growing ability to sympathize with others, which will seem incongruent with their seemingly selfish need to be first. The latter may be propelled by an emerging and not altogether unhealthy need to succeed.

We must not overlook the fact that a big piece of a Discover child's emotional sensitivity is the development of their conscience. Older Discover children are beginning to understand right from wrong and to feel guilty when they do something wrong. They are ready to receive the simplest, most uncluttered truths of the Gospel.

For example: "God loves us even though we do wrong. Everyone does wrong. Everyone needs a Saviour. Jesus is the Saviour we all need. God forgives the wrong we do because Jesus saves us from it."

Whenever your lesson presents an opportunity to talk about any part of the Gospel, welcome the children's questions. Offer to talk further with a child who wants to know more about asking Jesus to be their Saviour.

Socially. As Discover children begin to emerge into the bigger world around them, they become more aware of others.

---

17 See Appendix 6: Helping Parents Nurture Good Relationships with Their Children.

Connecting well with others becomes one of their primary developmental tasks and needs.

Sharing and taking turns will continue to be hard for them and they will change friends often, but they are beginning to choose best friends. Sometimes Discover boys will think girls have cooties and do everything they can to avoid them. Other times Discover boys and girls will form easy friendships with one another.

As important as friendships with their peers are to Discover children, friendships with significant adults in their lives are even more important. It's as if God designed Discover children for role-modelling relationships! They have a lot of respect for the grownups in their lives and desperately want their teachers' approval.

Show them that they are important to you. Use their names. Make the most of every opportunity to give them your warm and undivided attention. Remember the things they tell you about themselves and ask about these personal interests. Listen well when they talk. Set a good example by responding calmly and reassuringly to them and to things that happen. For example, "I know you both want to use the glue right now, but there's only one bottle. Instead of fighting over it, how can you work things out in a kind way?"

They will remember the overall feeling of an experience or relationship more than what is said. We will need God's help to get this right! When our response is not what it should be, we can model the right way to handle mistakes by asking both God and the children to forgive us. We will need God's help to forgive ourselves. Continuously turning to God for help, we can ask Him to fill us with His Holy Spirit so the children can see His patience and kindness in us.

Remember, too, that even though they still have a long way to go, Discover children want to be grown up like you. Avoid talking down to them and call them anything but "little." Let them help!

Helping not only allows Discover children to move about and become fully engaged; it's also the grown-up and godly thing to do!

Picture a young child in elementary school, afraid of the dark or nervous about her first piano recital. Instead of being overcome by fear, this child asks God for help and relaxes in the confidence that He is bigger than whatever makes her anxious. When this little girl is tempted to lie or take something that doesn't belong to her, she remembers that God has plainly said that lying and stealing are wrong. She chooses to obey God because she loves Him and wants to please Him. And in a world where so many of us are self-absorbed, this little girl is learning to be kind and generous like Jesus. She is learning to care about others.

Discover Trail Goals

- I Can Trust God
- Obedience Is Best
- Giving Is God's Way
- I Treat Others the Way I Would Like to Be Treated

Trail goals are meant to be cumulative. As the children age, continue to teach them the Trail goals of previous sections.

It may be helpful to imagine the connection between Welcome Circle, Wonder, and Discover goals in different ways.

In one possible metaphor, Welcome Circle and Wonder goals become the foundational blocks upon which we intentionally build Discover concepts. In another metaphor, Welcome Circle and Wonder goals become elastics that extend or stretch into Discover goals. Viewed yet another way, Welcome Circle and Wonder goals become the very air or atmosphere that permeate everything we teach in Discover.

For best results in your Discover ministry, ignore the proverbial caution not to mix metaphors! Intentionally weave earlier Trail goals with Discover goals any and every way you can.

I can trust God. Discover children are ready to trust God. They have lots of fears and plenty of questions. They want to trust those who are bigger and older than they are. They need to know that God *is* and that God, who is the biggest (all-powerful) and the wisest (all-knowing), is also always present to help them even when adults aren't or can't.

Moreover, Discover children need to know that God *will* help them, because this is who God is. God is love. God is good and God is giving. He is for us and not against us. He will always help, in His own wisest way, anyone and everyone who sincerely asks.

Open Bible stories as if they are treasure chests, ready to reveal the loving goodness of God. Look beyond the human characters in the story to God Himself. Bring every Bible story to God before you take it to the children. Ask Him how the story shows that He is Someone they can safely trust.

Pray with the children. Invite them to bring their specific fears to God and ask for His help. Encourage them to trust God's perfect timing and greater wisdom even when He doesn't help them exactly when or how they think He should.

Help strengthen children's faith in God by teaching them to thank God for the ways in which He has already helped them. Remind the children often that Jesus loves them and is their very best friend. Remind them, too, that they can talk to Jesus anywhere, anytime, about anything.

Prior to this age, children typically had adults pray over them or give them words to say to God. Encourage Discover children to use their own words when they talk to God. Remembering that children between the ages of five and eight tend to be shy and still have trouble expressing what they feel, reassure them that God hears the prayers we whisper as clearly as He hears the prayers we say out loud.

Discover children need to hear about your own experiences of trusting God. Journal your personal record of answered prayer and tell the children about these whenever it's appropriate. Discover more of the vast and trustworthy nature of God together!

Obedience is best. As we have seen, God awakens the conscience in children this age, but they still need caring adults to help them distinguish right from wrong. We aren't the authors of what is right. God is. Help the children learn what is right from God and then rely on His help to choose right over wrong in their daily lives.

For example, as children we have probably all been tempted to disobey loving instruction from caring parents. Children need to know that God cares about the choice they make in response to this temptation (Ephesians 6:1).

Obedience is integrally related to loving and trusting God. It's because we trust God's loving wisdom that we choose to obey Him. We trust Him to help us when it's hard to do what He wants us to do. We trust Him to forgive us when we don't obey Him.

Look for themes of faith and obedience in the Bible stories you tell. Point out the human examples in these stories, good and bad, but always emphasize the astounding goodness of God.

Discover children will love putting their newfound reading skills to work with the Bible. They are ready to see the Bible as a collection of books and will love finding page numbers for specific books of the Bible in the table of contents. Even though it will take them a while, they'll also enjoy using chapter and verse references to look up specific passages.

But part of teaching Discover children that obedience is best is to help them see the Bible as one story from cover to cover. This is the story of Jesus and God's redemptive plan for us. The price God was willing to pay for our redemption proves that He loves us and that His way is and always has been... best.

Giving is God's way. When you tell a Bible story, demonstrate that God is generous. Story after story shows God giving His undeserved favour (grace) and withholding the punishment we deserve (mercy). We see Him heal people, forgive people, and give people both His undivided time and attention and all kinds of practical things like oil, bread, and fish—lots and lots of fish!

Best of all, we see the way in which God gives us Jesus! But don't just talk about the way God gives; help the children follow His example.

Never underestimate a child's ability to give. Let Discover children help you and other children during your time together. Find ways to have Discover children contribute to intergenerational events. Can they welcome people at the door? Can they help bake and serve cookies?

Have Discover children craft gifts for members of their families and for younger children and seniors in their neighbourhood. Facilitate visits to senior homes for Discover children and their families. The smallest gifts, even a child's handmade card, when personally delivered, will bless an older person.

Look for ways to have the children give to others in their broader community. Invite them to collect and donate school supplies for immigrant children. One Discover teacher encouraged the children to donate toys they had outgrown to a local used toy drive.

Discover children can also lead the way in expressing gratitude to community heroes: teachers at school, firefighters, police officers, nurses, and others. Combine giving with more discovering.

For example, when you take handmade thank-you cards and/or snacks to firefighters, arrange to take a tour of the fire station.

Teach the children, too, to give out of their abundance to people who have far less in other parts of the world. Include mission lessons in your curriculum. If your church is partnering with a church in another part of the world, draw the children into the partnership, keeping them up-to-date on the work the churches are doing together, introducing them to people in your partner church, and leading the children to pray for these people and their specific needs. Encourage the children to give some of their own money and/or spearhead a fundraising project.

Consider enhancing your Discover curriculum with mission lessons for children. The easiest and most effective way to do this might be to teach these mission lessons four or five Sundays in a row.

In other words, designate a month for missions! I like May because of the alliteration, and because by May regular Discover teachers are usually ready for a break. Give them a break by recruiting experienced missionaries or mission-minded people to take turns teaching missions for a month of Sundays.

I treat others the way I would like to be treated. As children this age step into a greater awareness of people around them, they are ready to discover God's way of making good connections. Learning God's way of treating others the way we would like to be treated will help children nurture strong and healthy relationships the rest of their lives.

Open Bible stories to show the children how Jesus treated people. Talk about what Jesus did and said. Ask, "What do you think Jesus meant? How do you think Jesus felt when He said/did that? How did it make the other person/people feel? If you had been there, what do you think Jesus would have said to you? How would that make you feel? What would you say to Jesus?"

Jesus tells us to love one another. With His profound understanding of our human limitations, He makes this easier to grasp with this simple instruction: *"Love your neighbor as yourself"* (Matthew 19:19).

Jesus knows that even though we are each a unique creation of God, we are all the same in our humanity. We all have the same kind of emotional and relational needs. So He tells us that when we treat others the way we want to be treated, we will be doing well.

How do we all want to be treated? We all want to be treated with kindness. We all want to be accepted just as we are. We all want to belong. We all want to be encouraged and comforted, given a chance to try and permission to fail. We all want to be forgiven. We all want to be loved.

We can turn ordinary, real-life moments into opportunities to help children grasp this spiritual concept. When two children begin to argue over taking turns, ask, "What would you want someone to do for you if you hadn't had a turn?" When someone has an accident ask, "What would you want other people to do if you dropped the crayons?" If someone speaks when someone else is talking, ask, "If you were trying to tell a story, what would you want the other children to do?"

All of Discover is an opportunity to learn how to relate to people God's way!

Discover Curriculum

Choosing from the many options of published curricula for early elementary children has been one of the most challenging aspects of children's ministry for me. There are so many choices! Each seems to promise something they think is lacking in the others.

But the best Discover lessons aren't lifted directly off the pages of a published curriculum. The best lessons come from the God-inspired hearts and giftedness of dedicated teachers.

Still, God uses published lessons to inspire good teachers. A published lesson provides the foundational outline and a potpourri of ideas for teachers to use. This contribution is significant.

You may want to write a lesson from scratch from time to time, but trying to develop a full-blown curriculum of your own will take valuable time and energy away from teaching. Our teaching will be enriched by the published writers' expertise. Published lessons are designed by experts—in theology, pedology, technology, and every other ology we need!

How do we find the curriculum that will help us most? After scanning the material for major red flags such as unsound theology or age-inappropriateness, look for lesson designs that:

- help the children discover Jesus and fall in love with Him.
- help the children see the difference that a biblical truth makes in real life. Does the curriculum show the children how Jesus can help them with their five- to eight-year-old choices, problems, and needs? When they hear the main truth of a lesson, children should be able to answer the question: "So what?"
- supply a variety of learning activities to help engage every child. Look for learning activities that facilitate open-ended discussion, student expression (not the teacher's), and discovery! Does each lesson include visual (sight), auditory (listening), tactile (touching), and kinesthetic (moving) learning activities? We all learn best by engaging all our senses, but children this age are also beginning to have a preferred learning style.

Being able to choose, even if it's just between two options, is important to them. Video games tend to be overstimulating and addictive, but they appeal to a child's appetite for challenge, problem-solving, and making their own choices.
- encourage children to step into the real-life experiences of ministry, mission, and giving.
- nurture relationships. Do the lessons encourage the children to become friends with one another and with good role models? Most importantly, does the curriculum nurture a meaningful relationship with Jesus?

What to look for in published curricula. Look for a written layout that is well organized and easy for teachers to follow.

Larry Richards, a Christian education specialist whose textbooks I studied when I was in seminary back in the 1970s, suggested we divide our lesson plan into four parts. He named these four parts: Hook, Book, Look, and Took.[18]

When you look at a lesson, keep your eye out for:

- Hook: a thought that connects something in a child's previous experience with the main biblical truth or story.
- Book: a Bible story written in an age-appropriate way, along with creative ideas for telling it.
- Look: thoughtful questions and activities that help the child look deeper into the Bible story to grasp and apply the main truth. For example, instead of adding crafts, just because they're fun and keep the children occupied, are there crafts that either remind the child

---

18 Lawrence O. Richards, *Creative Bible Teaching* (Chicago, IL: Moody Press, 1970), 108–114.

of the main truth or help the child share that truth with someone else?
- Took: real-life experiences that help the child apply the main biblical truth.

Also look for media resources such as screen alternatives for storytelling and music with sign language and other motions. Music helps us remember. Choose songs that teach a Bible truth and/or a passage of Scripture.

An effective curriculum will also come with easy-to-apply ideas for parents that can be sent home to extend the child's learning experience through the week.

What to avoid in published curricula. There are a few dangers—besides poor theology, age-inappropriateness, and too much "teacher talking"—to avoid in the curriculum we choose.

These include material that is designed for the head and not the heart. Avoid information-focused curricula that may increase a child's knowledge about the Bible but do little to help the child discover Jesus and fall in love with Him. The curriculum may or may not suggest ways to create spaces that help the children be with Jesus. If these aren't included in the curriculum you use, you can add them.

For example, call the children to stillness. Explain that we can light a candle to remind us that God is right here with us. Lead them in a quiet song that helps them think about Jesus. Encourage them to close their eyes and talk to Jesus about something they're feeling or thinking about.

Avoid questions that require one correct answer. Curriculum questions that merely help the child review the facts of a Bible story without leading them into a deeper reflection of the biblical truth tend to hide the revelation of God.

For example, avoid asking, "How many fish and loaves of bread did Jesus use to feed the crowd?" Instead ask, "What do you think is the most amazing thing that happened in this story?" Open-ended questions lead to greater spiritual formation and protect children from the pressure they sometimes feel to come up with the correct answer.

Also steer clear of lessons that are moralistic and behaviour-oriented instead of focused on the characteristics of God and the powerful, life-transforming good news about Jesus.

For example, consider the story of Jesus waking up in the boat and calming the waves and the sea. When we tell that story, we may be tempted to focus on the disciples' lack of faith and implore the children to have more faith. If we taught the lesson that way, we would be morally and spiritually correct, but that focus masks the magnificent authority and power Jesus demonstrated. Instead teach this main truth: Jesus is even more powerful than wind and waves.

It's also wise to avoid lessons that rely on crazy games and gimmicks, silly music, and overly energetic leaders to get kids excited and wanting to keep coming back. It's not that we can't have fun. In fact, Discover should be lots of fun!

But as Jack Klumpenhower points out, crazy games and gimmicks, silly music, and overly energetic leaders get kids excited about these things themselves. Shouldn't we be showing them Jesus so they can get excited about Him? When we use other things to keep kids interested, we tend to show them Jesus as a sideline. The subtle message is that these other things are more exciting than He is.[19]

Klumpenhower goes on to say that many people who grow up in the church "never see Jesus so strikingly that He becomes their overriding hope and their greatest love. They are never convinced

---

19 Jack Klumpenhower, *Show Them Jesus: Teaching the Gospel to Kids* (Greensboro, NC: New Growth Press, 2014), 155.

that Jesus is better, a zillion times better, than anything and everything else."[20]

Explore curricula options, and ask other children's ministry workers which curriculum they use. How do they describe its pros and cons?

Take a closer look at two or three curriculum options. Do they have serious dangers to avoid? How many helpful elements do they include? One curriculum may not supply everything that's helpful, but it's generally easier to help your teachers find extra resources than avoid inherent dangers.

Disciplining Discover Kids

Disciplining Discover kids is a lot like fitting together pieces of a jigsaw puzzle. The beautiful picture of disciplining a child is made up of at least five significant pieces fitted together and framed in a loving, caring relationship:

- Understanding discipline.
- Preparing lessons.
- Setting clear and consistent boundaries.
- Utilizing engaged helpers.
- Responding to individual needs.

Understanding discipline. So much of what we think of as discipline is us reacting to behaviour that threatens our need to be in control.

A child constantly makes side cracks to his buddy while we're telling the Bible story. The two boys aren't disturbing the other children, but we feel indignant that they aren't respecting the

---

20 Ibid., 4.

rule against talking while others are talking. By trying to control them, we keep interrupting ourselves to shush them.

If we're self-aware enough to realize it, we might see that we feel personally threatened by the boys' seeming lack of interest. We wonder, isn't our storytelling captivating enough to keep their attention?

In another instance, we may feel frustrated with a distressed child who constantly interrupts the session with tears and pleas for attention. We impatiently send her to a timeout so we can stay in control of the lesson.

Discipline is not about us. It's not even about our awesome, or less-than-awesome, lesson plan. Discipline also isn't about us reacting to behaviour that threatens and frustrates us. Nor is it about punishing or controlling a child's behaviour.

Discipline is about us responding to a child's needs. It's about us trying to understand what the child is thinking and feeling so we can respond in all the right ways and help the child respond in all the right ways. It's about guiding a child's behaviour and helping them make good choices.

The word "discipline" comes from the same root as the word "disciple." Like discipling, disciplining is positive, nurturing guidance and teaching. Understanding a Discover child's needs and responding in calm, loving ways with the right kind of discipline is even more important than the lesson plan!

Preparing lessons. Even a little experience in Discover ministry shows us that a good lesson well prepared reduces behaviour problems. If the main biblical truth of a lesson is clear and easy to grasp, if the Hook, Book, Look, and Took parts of the lesson are enhanced with creative visual, auditory, tactile, and kinaesthetic experiences, if the children are encouraged to participate, and if the leader can move the learning experience along without having to interrupt themselves to go get missing items, etc., then there won't be any time for the children to misbehave!

Always have more planned and prepared than you think you'll need so the children can stay happily engaged until their parents arrive to pick them up.

We often race past a critical part of lesson preparation. Perhaps we neglect this critical piece because it seems less urgent than physical preparations. Or maybe we ignore it because even though we give intellectual assent to our need for God's help, our true self tends to operate out of a sense of self-sufficiency.

The truth is that we are helpless and ineffective without God. We need to invite God into our lesson design and sessions, into our relationships with the children, and into ourselves. Only as He fills us with His Holy Spirt and gives us His love, patience, and wisdom will we be able to respond to the children in all the right ways.

Setting clear and consistent boundaries. Boundaries, or guardrails, are the rules we put in place for the group. Discover rules should be few and simple. They should be practical expressions of two basic principles: be safe and help others be safe, and be kind so others can learn.

Talk with the children about these principles in your first session, and frequently afterward. Children need to know how we expect them to behave and why.

Ask the children to suggest specific rules that can help keep everyone safe and able to learn.[21] For example, when it comes to safety, they might consider how we may distract or hurt others with our hands and suggest a specific rule like "Hands are for helping." To help us be kind so others can learn, the rule might be that children are to raise their hand in the air and stop talking when they see the leader raise their hand in the air.

---

[21] Jody Capehart, Gordon West, and Becki West, *The Discipline Guide for Children's Ministry* (Loveland, CO: Group, 1997), 79–80.

Once the children agree on a few simple rules that will help keep them all safe and able to learn, print the rules and post them where the children can see them. Expect the children to obey them. Remind the children of the rules and the principles behind them when you guide and correct their behaviour.

Utilizing engaged helpers. When it comes to managing children's behaviour, it's always helpful to reduce the number of children in each group and increase the adult-child ratio.

However, it isn't enough to simply have more helpers in the room. Helpers should be trained to anticipate the leader's needs and do all they can to keep the leader from being interrupted.

Even more importantly, helpers are frontline workers when it comes to meeting the children's needs. Even the best teachers can't accomplish much without good helpers—and without good helpers, children can be overlooked and neglected.

One way to raise a helper's sense of responsibility may be to let them teach parts of the lesson while the main leader models what it looks like to be an effective helper. I learned most of what I know about being a good helper from an older, more experienced teacher who taught the concepts in a workshop and then modelled them in a session I was leading.

Discover helpers do all they can to help the children stay focused on the lesson. Sometimes a helper quiets the children merely by sitting with them in their group. Sometimes a helper settles a restless child simply by making eye contact. Other times, they help by giving a disruptive child a gentle touch on the shoulder or arm.

In one Discover session, a helper may find it works best to position themselves between two children who are distracting each other. In another session, they may find it works best for them to stay on their feet and move around the group, settling restless children with a loving look or gentle touch as needed. The helper participates in the lesson with the children, following the leader's directives and encouraging the children to follow them, too.

A good helper does everything they can to protect the leader from interruptions. When a child arrives late or when someone shows up at the door, the helper goes to the door so the leader can continue working with the group. When a child needs to use the washroom, it is one of the helpers who goes with the child. When a child needs one-on-one attention, it is initially the helper who takes the child aside to talk; if they can't calm or help the child, they take the child to a more experienced helper or the leader.

Helpers also join the children in their small group learning activities. They use this less structured time to nurture loving relationships with the children and help them have fun. They come alongside new children to help them understand what's happening. They not only help children with the learning activity, they also help children think it through by talking with them about the activity and helping them make connections with the lesson's main truth.

If a child won't engage in any of the learning activities, the helper makes sure the child at least stays in the room. Some children don't have any boundaries at home. Knowing there are lines they cannot cross at church gives them an otherwise-missing sense of security. When a child needs to be physically restrained, stop them by putting your hands on their shoulders.

Traditionally we have thought of Discover volunteers as teacher's helpers. They do help the teacher, but just as importantly they help the children. Good helpers are indispensable to both.

Responding to individual needs. Because our thoughts and feelings tend to affect the way we behave, especially when we're children, it is important to understand what a child is thinking and feeling. When it comes to guiding and correcting their behaviour, there are several ways to find out what a child is thinking and feeling. It helps to follow a process of elimination.

Understanding a child's personality or learning style can provide important clues. The incorrigible child who rushes from one thing to another may be bored and need a challenge. The child who stays against the wall refusing to participate may feel inadequate and need to be encouraged.

All children, like the rest of us, do better with lots of sincere affirmation. Getting to know the children and understanding their personalities will help us guide and correct their behaviour.

It's also important to understand, without attaching labels, any special needs the child may have. Children with Attention Deficient Disorder, for example, need calming with a quiet demeanour and gentle humour. Give simple, specific instructions to refocus their attention on the task at hand.

Perhaps the most obvious way to understand what a child is thinking and feeling is to talk with the child. Train your helpers to have at least an initial conversation with the child who has misbehaved. Teach your helpers to take the child aside, squat to make eye contact, and speak with them quietly and lovingly. Sometimes a child is out of sorts because they're hungry, tired, or feeling physically unwell. Starting with inquiries about these less complicated needs may give us enough understanding. If it doesn't, questions like "What did you have for breakfast this morning?" and "Do you hurt anywhere?" will communicate care and invite the child to reveal the real problem.

Train your helpers to let the child speak first and then listen to the child's thoughts and feelings as though the child was the only person in the room. Encourage your helpers to empathize with the child's feelings, reinforce right ways of thinking, and help the child to choose better ways of behaving.

If, for example, a child reacts in anger because they were left out of a game, we can tell them we understand how they feel but then ask them why the way they acted was inappropriate. Ask,

"What would be a better choice to make next time you feel that way?" If the child continues to willfully disobey after the talk about making better choices, let them experience reasonable consequences for the wrong choices they have made. For example, if they continue to misuse an object, take the object away from them. If they misbehave in a game, remove them from the game.

Timeouts can too easily become a default consequence for misbehaving. Too often we go right to the timeout without trying to understand the child's needs. When time alone in a corner is used as punishment, it can feel very unloving and lonely.

But quiet spaces designed to help a child calm themselves will nurture feelings of love and caring. Put a comfy beanbag chair in your "quiet corner." Hang a mirror or nature scene on the wall. Encourage the child to be in the moment by taking deep breaths. Give them a stress ball to squeeze. The child may want to focus on a puzzle, or some other tactile activity, and they may want you to help them with it.[22]

Sometimes children won't be able to tell us what they're thinking and feeling. They may be afraid to put their thoughts and feelings into words, or their thoughts and feelings may be too complicated for them to understand.

You may want to ask an experienced teacher to observe the child and give you advice. Meanwhile, find ways to comfort the child. Take the child to the quiet corner for some one-on-one time and then accompany them when they return to their learning activity. Or send for one of the child's parents to come and be with them.

Talk privately with the parent, asking for insights into the child's behaviour and how to manage it. Use "I" language. For example, say, "I'm having a problem understanding how to help *(child's name)* when they get upset. What works at home?" Partner with the

---

[22] Emily Snider, "Mindfulness," *Children's Ministry Magazine*, September-October 2017.

parent to find solutions. Offer to go with the parent if it seems wise to consult the child's schoolteacher and/or other professionals.

Some final words of advice would be Winston Churchill's: "Never, never give up!" No matter how difficult a child may be, love them enough to never give up on them.

Once, my ministry team almost gave up on a Discover child whose behaviour was extremely difficult. By God's grace, we didn't. When the child was just a little bit older, this same child announced that they liked being at church because it was a place where they felt safe and loved.

Launch

Trail Section Four: *Preteens*

When I was nine years old, a Brownie in my "six" was struck by a car and killed. My mom suggested we pay our respects at the funeral home. She thought if I wore my Brownie uniform, it would help the family know why I was there.

I must have been apprehensive, but I don't remember being afraid. What I remember is the shock I felt when I looked into the casket and saw that they had dressed the other little girl in her Brownie uniform.

"That could have been me," I thought, realizing for the first time that I might not grow old before I died.

Suddenly I desperately wanted to know that things were right between God and me. Since my family went to church every Sunday, I began to listen very carefully to the pastor. I grasped enough of the Gospel to know that Jesus is the One who makes things right between God and me and I put my faith in Him.

About the Name

THE FOURTH SECTION OF THE TRAIL, DESIGNED FOR UPPER ELEMENTARY children or preteens, is called Launch. It's all about launching kids into adolescence.

As we continue to nurture preteens spiritually, our goal is to help them become safely anchored in a personal relationship with Jesus, and in God's perspective on the various issues that will become increasingly relevant to them as teenagers. Safely anchored in God and His Word, they will be paradoxically free, like a kite, to soar above a lot of the turbulence of their teen years.

Our society acknowledges that adolescence, the transition from childhood to adulthood, can be fraught with danger. But we rarely hear anyone talk about providing spiritual help for it.

Yet it is life in and with God that makes every part of us well and whole. Holiness is wholeness.

Launch provides an exciting and critical opportunity to join God in forming lives and leaders for His Kingdom purposes. God is able to do immeasurably more than we can imagine with even one preteen who is intentionally and spiritually launched from preadolescence into the rest of their life.

About Launch Kids

Every preteen has a God-given uniqueness, and we will want to know and appreciate that uniqueness. Furthermore, they all develop at their own rate and have already had enough life experience to make them individually different from their peers.

Still, just as our humanity makes us more similar than we are different, there are developmental characteristics that give preadolescents some general cognitive, physical, emotional, and social similarities.

Cognitively. Kids this age tend to be sharp logical thinkers. We can say to them, "If this, then that," and they get it.

So help them think about Scripture. Keep them engaged and challenged so they don't get bored. Let them read a passage and then use their own words to tell you and others what they got out of it.

Preteens thrive on interacting with others, so create lots of lively discussion. They are also highly creative. As with younger children, let them use not just words but also visual art and imaginative projects to express themselves. Encourage them to ask questions about things that don't make logical sense while endorsing the mystery of all things spiritual.

For example, you could engage with them about the fact that Jesus fed five thousand people with two small loaves of bread and five fish. This may not make sense logically, but it's an example of the mysterious power of God.

Part of launching preteens into adolescence is launching them into the realm of spiritual mystery and faith. This is a realm of reality that surpasses logic.

The world of truth is so vast and eternal that it cannot be contained in or controlled by our finite reasoning. What a relief it is to realize that God and His truth are so much bigger and greater than what we can see and comprehend!

Only God can help us begin to grasp what we cannot see; only God can help us travel the road of sound reasoning as far as it will go, and then meet us at the edge to lift us safely into the deep knowing of the soul.

Ask God to give your kids faith. Tell them about specific ways God has done this for you. It's also okay to admit that we don't have all the answers and that some things may have to remain a mystery this side of heaven.

When your Launch kids ask questions and sound doubtful, don't panic! Realize that doubt is not the opposite of faith; doubt is the way to faith. Create a safe space for lots of discussion, and centre that discussion in God's Word.

Many preteens are able to think abstractly. God can speak to them through illustrations, word pictures, and other people's real-life experiences.

They are ready to hear God speak to them through the parables He told and through the names He has given Himself to describe the kind of relationship He wants to have with them—for example: Shepherd, Fortress, Light of the World, Bread of Life, Living Water, etc.

This is a great time to lift biblical heroes like David, Daniel, Esther, Hannah, Peter, Paul, and Mary off the pages of Scripture to help the kids know them as real people. Introduce preteens to other great heroes of the Christian faith as well, such as John Bunyan, Florence Nightingale, Martin Luther, Harriet Tubman, and J. Hudson Taylor. There are so many others!

Preteens are curious. Introduce them to credible sources of information, like Bible concordances, Bible dictionaries, and safe websites. But remember that kids this age aren't interested in busy-work. Let them research issues that are part of their day-to-day experience. For example, encourage them to watch YouTube videos or visit websites about bullying.

Physically. Upper elementary children grow and change at different rates. Girls tend to mature physically faster than boys. Many girls start their menstrual cycle at this age and are taller than boys. Tall or short, plump or thin, preteens tend to feel self conscious and sensitive about their appearance and can feel awkward about the way their bodies are changing. Add hormones and consequent mood swings to the mix and you've got kids who can feel vulnerable and out of control a lot of the time.

Preteens move fast with astounding amounts of energy, but they tire easily. When they're tired, they can feel listless and/or irritable and have trouble controlling their tongues and other impulses.

When they aren't tired, Launch kids are physically fast and accurate. They love organized games and large group activities. When you do play games with them, remember that they have a strong sense of fair play, so be consistent with the rules.

Emotionally. All the physical changes they're experiencing make preteens emotionally sensitive. It's no wonder that bigger life challenges, and even just things that go wrong in the run of a day, can leave them emotionally drained. Caring adults can help restore a preteen's emotional equilibrium by listening carefully and sensitively when a preteen wants to share.

Because they struggle with low self-esteem, it's especially important not to criticize or belittle preteens. Be careful not to label them, not even in your own mind!

If discipline problems persist, ask gentle questions to understand the child's need and help them understand how their actions affect others. Remember that anger and angry actions are often fuelled by more hidden thoughts and feelings.

Ask God to help you remember how you felt when you were their age. Ask Him to give you compassion for the preteen's feelings of inadequacy, rejection, and uncertainty. Talk with the preteen soon after a difficult conversation to assure them that they can still feel safe and natural with you.

Launch kids tend to have lots of fears and anxieties. The worries they had as they emerged into life as Discover children can persist and intensify during the preteen years as even more of their childhood protection falls away.

Many of their worries stem from their personal feelings of inadequacy. For example, "How well am I doing at school? How much do my friends like me?" Other fears revolve around issues they cannot control either in their own families or in society generally. For example, "What if one of my parents dies? What do I do about the drugs and drinking around me?"

Today we could undoubtedly add violence and war, racism, natural disasters, climate change, pandemics, and other traumatic events—all current realities that get lots of airtime in the news and on social media.

Socially. Best friends are very important to kids at this age. The need to be accepted by their peers is a natural part of the process of gaining independence from their parents. Having even just one bestie—a friend who accepts and likes them, shares some of their interests, and remains loyal to them—can help preteens navigate a lot of pressure.

Consequently, one of the most important things we can do for preteens is provide a safe place to gather with others their age and form loving, supportive friendships. It's especially helpful for kids with faith and biblical values to have like-minded friends.

Some kids are beginning to be interested in the opposite sex, but the LGBTQ+ community has made us aware that some may be struggling with same-sex attraction or their gender identity. If Launch kids aren't wrestling with their own sexual orientation or gender identity issues, they will know people who are. It's a conversation waiting to happen. We all need help with the conversation and may want to turn to professionals for guidance. But unless we accept every preteen just as they are and love them as unconditionally as God does, hard conversations with them are doomed to fail. Our job is to love and listen, introduce preteens to Jesus, and provide a safe place where they can bring their questions.

To become independent adults, kids transitioning from childhood to adulthood must find their identity apart from their parents. Kids with a strong sense of belonging in their family aren't as apt to experiment with extreme identities. But even preteens with a healthy sense of belonging are now old enough to realize that they are an individual apart from their parents and other family members. They are ready to discover their unique identity.

They need help with this. Most preteens, when left to themselves, will try to resolve their identity crisis by looking to others to tell them who they should be. Consequently, they're often pulled into peer subcultures that are defined by music, dress, speech, attitudes, actions, etc.

Another natural part of growing up is wanting to be independent. What preteens don't always realize is that responsibility is an inherent part of independence. Launch kids need our help to learn and accept responsibility. And we, together with their parents, need to learn to give them responsibility gradually, trust them with it, and let them fail, learn from their mistakes, and keep trying.

Even small successes build self-confidence. Because so many of a preteen's needs are enmeshed in their relationship with their parents, Launch, at its core, is a ministry to both preteens and their parents.

Preteens want to be active. They want to be doing rather than watching and they want to be doing things that truly make a difference. They love a challenge and can emphasize with others. Launch kids are ripe for service and mission projects.

Imagine a preteen living in the ambiguous place between childhood and adulthood, unable to look at life with the innocence of a child yet not ready to deal with its adult-sized problems.

As they approach adolescence, preteens are filled with anxiety-riddled questions. "Who am I? Does anyone like me? Do I like me? How can I find my way through problems at school, at home, or anywhere else?"

Now imagine a group of caring adults and older youth coming alongside that distraught preadolescent and saying, "We like you and we love you. But most importantly, you are the apple of God's eye. He delights in you! The key to managing life is to respond to God's love by loving Him and depending on Him. He will help you accept and like yourself. He will help you grow into all that He wants you to be. We will look to Him together for help with life's problems and challenges."

Launch Trail Goals

- Understand Adolescence
- Choose Jesus
- Begin Spiritual Disciplines
- Serve Others

Welcome, Wonder, and Discover goals form a strong and firm foundation for everything Launch kids need in order to know and understand about God. Have a look at some of the ways these previous goals address a preteen's cognitive, physical, emotional, and social needs:

- God Made Me: I am wonderfully and fearfully made. God knew what He was doing when He made me, and He has plans for me.
- Jesus Loves Me: Jesus thinks I'm wonderful and only wants what's best for me.
- Church Is a Happy Place to Be: I can be myself with the people at my church. I feel safe there.
- Church Is a Family for My Family: The people at my church are like an extended family for me and my family. They care about me and my family and will help us.
- God Made Everything: The world didn't just happen. God created it and all that is awesome and good in it. There is nothing God cannot do. God wants me to help Him take care of the world He made.
- Jesus Is My Best Friend: Jesus is both my sovereign Lord and my Bestie. I am never alone. He understands me and loves me no matter what. He helps me with all my problems.

- I Can Talk to Jesus Anywhere, Anytime, About Anything: I can be perfectly honest with God about everything I'm thinking and feeling. He loves it when I talk with Him. It means I believe in Him.
- The Bible Is God's Special Book: The Bible helps me know God, what He thinks about me, and what He thinks about life. I can read the Bible for myself and get help to understand it.
- I Can Trust God: Even though I can't see Him with my eyes, I know He's there and on my side. I can ask for His help with absolutely anything and get it, but not always the way I expect.
- Obedience Is Best: Making choices God wants me to make is the only way to truly succeed with life and enjoy it!
- Giving Is God's Way: Getting stuff only makes me happy for a while. Giving to others is so much more satisfying. I want to help and serve others the way Jesus did.
- I Treat Others the Way I Want To Be Treated: Relationships are hard, and it seems like I'm always messing them up. God can help me with this. It helps to know other people have the same feelings I have.

It's important to weave these basic Trail goals and concepts into everything we teach in Launch, both for preteens who are entering the faith community for the first time and for kids who have grown up in the church and learned them before.

Launch kids who grew up in church are now ready to absorb basic truths at a much deeper level. But we are also ready to add new spiritual goals and concepts designed to help kids with specific preadolescent challenges.

Understand adolescence. A critical part of the Launch ministry is helping preteens understand that the changes they're going through, and will go through, are normal.

At Launch, we assure preteens that it's normal and inevitable—reassurance for late bloomers!—that their bodies will change as they move from childhood into adulthood. We explore the ways these changes affect them emotionally and assure them that they aren't alone in their struggle to accept and like themselves. We open God's Word and show them that God not only formed them in their mother's womb but is also with them orchestrating their transition into adulthood (Psalm 139:13–16).

We also talk openly with preteens about their need to figure out who they are. We give them lots of opportunities to do new things so they can discover their personal aptitudes and abilities.

We affirm the competencies and potential we see in them. Even more importantly, we open God's Word and show them that they are first and foremost someone God has created, and that God has plans and purposes for their lives (Jeremiah 29:11). We open God's Word and show them that their first and greatest purpose is to have a close, personal relationship with God (Matthew 22:37–38). We help them find their identity as a totally accepted and dearly loved child of God (1 John 3:1).

We talk with preteens, too, about their natural desire and need to become independent. We teach them how to honour their parents by assuming more responsibility on their journey to independence. We coach them as we gradually release more responsibility to them in Launch.

And we become a safe forum where troublesome issues raised by their personal life experiences and frightening headlines can be named, unpacked, and addressed by God's Word. Preteens are already thinking about things we would rather they didn't know about. We will need God's help to speak of these matters humbly, bravely, and with sensitivity.

Make Parent Night a regular Launch event. Use special speakers or choose creative ways to explore pertinent topics with both preteens and their parents. Line up topics and speakers in advance so you can give parents plenty of time to put Parent Nights in their calendars. Help parents feel welcome and comfortable when they come. Plan icebreakers and schedule time for them to mingle with the kids and other parents. Respect the questions and contributions every parent makes to the discussion. Whenever possible, provide resources for parents.

Another way to help Launch kids into adolescence is to work closely with youth group leaders, supporting them and encouraging them in their ministry with teens and partnering with them to help preteens cross the gap into youth ministry. Invite youth leaders to Launch. Let them hang out with the preteen kids, play games with them, and get to know them.

Ask youth leaders and mature teens and young adults to visit Launch and talk with your preteens about some of the issues on your need-to-discuss list. Kids will gravitate toward the oldest person in the room who truly loves them, but they'll really sit up and listen when someone just a little older than they are speaks about learning to navigate the problems most on a preteen's mind. An older teen, for example, can explain to the kids how they are learning to enact safe boundaries around social media and other digital challenges. Ask your Launch kids to submit questions ahead of time so your teen speaker has time to work with an adult mentor to prepare their responses.

Work with youth leaders to design a youth group night for kids in the spring before they join youth group. Your preteens will find it easier to join youth group the following fall if they've already been there and know what to expect. Help Launch kids transition into youth group by connecting them with other kids who are going. Arrange transportation.

Choose Jesus. Even though a child of any age can give everything they know about themselves to everything they know about Jesus, preteens have specific developmental needs that only Jesus can truly satisfy.

Whether or not they can say it in words, they are longing for Someone to accept and love them unconditionally. They are longing for a Best Friend who will never desert them and always understand what they're thinking and feeling. They are looking for forgiveness for their sins and mistakes they make. They want to know that things are good between them and God. They are looking for hope in a dark world, healing for their personal pain, and the promise that a time is coming when everything will be better. And whether they can articulate it or not, they want Someone to show them the way through all the choices that lie ahead.

Preteens can understand that God created them to be in a close relationship with Him, and they can recognize the sin and brokenness in them that keeps this from happening. They can know they can't fix this sin and brokenness themselves. They can see that they need a Saviour. They can also study the Scriptures that identify Jesus as the Saviour they need. They can know that God made Himself small enough to come into our brokenness and save us from it because He loves us too much to lose us. God's Holy Spirit can help preteens realize that they receive such a tremendous salvation by faith alone. He can also help them respond with a grateful desire to make Jesus the Leader or Lord of their lives.

The first and most important thing we can do to help preteens choose Jesus is to pray for them, fervently and faithfully. Only God can touch people at the point of their need and draw them to Him (John 6:44). Pray for your Launch kids and invite others to pray for them, too. Consider matching Launch kids with prayer warriors in your faith community who can also be their friends and role models.

Another important thing we can do to help preteens choose Jesus is to help them see Him! Rather than using the Bible to teach virtues and morals, lift the Gospel narrative and stories about Jesus out of the Bible. Help Launch kids step into the stories. Encourage them to use their imagination to picture themselves in the story with Jesus. Ask, "What do you notice about Jesus? What are people like when they're with Him? What is He saying to them? How is He helping them? What do you think He wants to say to you? What do you want to say to Jesus?"

Yet another critical dynamic in helping preteens (or anybody) choose Jesus is to bring them into close contact with people who trust Jesus to be their Saviour and follow Him as the Leader of their lives. What kids need most at this age are role models who show that trusting and following Jesus delivers what's promised, that Jesus truly is the Healer, Helper, and Hope we need Him to be.

The same Larry Richards who gave us the Hook/Book/Look/Took lesson outline and the seven principles for effective role-modelling[23] also gave us the following helpful insight into faith conversions.

In his book *Youth Ministry*, Richards describes something I have dubbed "a test for reality."[24] When we tell preadolescents (and others) that something about God, Jesus, or salvation is true, they are inclined to put it through a test for reality before they absorb it into their belief system. It's as though they hold the premise at arm's length until they spot the proof of it being true in someone else's life. Then they are more inclined to take it into their own life.

---

23 See Appendix 4: Larry Richards's Seven Principles for Effectively Role-Modelling.
24 Lawrence O. Richards, *Youth Ministry: Its Renewal in the Church* (Grand Rapids, MI: Zondervan, 1972), 179–182.

God often uses a test for reality to help kids new to the Gospel believe in it. He also often uses a test for reality to help kids who have grown up in a Christian family and/or faith community process their faith. It's natural and even necessary for preteens to detach from what their parents and faith community believe and put these beliefs through a test for reality before they own the beliefs themselves.

Authentic believers don't have to be perfect, nor can they be, for God to use them as effective role models. It's God showing up in their lives that makes the difference. Effective role models nurture their personal relationship with God, leaning into Him and the realities of the salvation He has given them in Jesus. The more consistently their lives match what they say they believe, the more effective they will be.[25]

As you make Jesus known, consistently invite Launch kids to choose Him to be their Saviour and the One in charge of their lives. Make it clear that it's a decision they have to make for themselves. Assure them that they can ask Jesus to come into their life to be their Saviour and Lord anytime, anywhere (Joel 2:32, Romans 10:13). Invite them to come to you if they want to talk about it. Explain that talking with someone about their decision helps make it feel more settled and real (Romans 10:9).

Begin spiritual disciplines. With our help, Launch kids can begin to include at least four spiritual disciplines in the rhythms of their daily, weekly, and monthly lives. You may want to introduce them to other spiritual disciplines, but these core four are especially timely for teens:

- spending personal quiet time alone with God each day.
- worshipping with the faith community every week.

---

25 See Appendix 4: Larry Richards's Seven Principles for Effectively Role-Modelling.

- studying the Bible with others every week.
- taking Jesus to others through missional service.

We help them start down these roads by taking small first steps.

Small first steps are especially appropriate when it comes to helping preteens start having their own daily devotions. Kids this age have outgrown having their parents read them a bedtime Bible story, so this is a natural time to hand the responsibility for daily Bible reading over to them. Supply preteens with an age-appropriate devotion book that explains a short passage of Scripture and suggests a topic for prayer. Find fun and creative ways to help them build the good habit of daily devotions. Expect kids to need "training wheels" for this spiritual discipline for at least three months.

In one of our churches, we helped Launch kids with the weekly spiritual disciplines of worship and Bible study by linking a weeknight Launch (we chose Friday night) to what was happening at church on Sunday mornings. Launch kids participated in intergenerational worship with the rest of the faith community on Sunday mornings and then slipped out for their own age-appropriate Bible study. Sometimes they stayed with the rest of the faith community for an extended intergenerational experience. Once a month, our preteens re-entered the sanctuary for communion, which was typically served at the end of the adult service.

Although we aimed to lead the kids into missional service every six to eight weeks, we couldn't always make the opportunities fit neatly into our calendar of events. Sometimes a longer period of time passed between projects, but we worked away at these as consistently and intentionally as we could.

Serve others. Whenever you lead kids into missional service, show them the biblical principles behind what they're doing. For example, when you take Launch kids to visit seniors, show them passages of Scripture that honour the elderly (Psalm 92:14, Isaiah

46:4). Before you take them to shop for the food bank, talk with them about ways we can share our abundance with others who have less (2 Corinthians 9:6–15).

Encourage the kids to actively look for God during these experiences. Afterwards give them an opportunity to talk about "God-sightings"—and their thoughts, feelings, and any questions they might have.

One of the key dynamics of Launch ministry is ministering *with* the kids. Their service may sometimes be loud, and it may sometimes be messy, but they have enough energy and just-do-it conviction to spread a passion for missional service throughout a church!

Launch Curriculum

If you have both a weeknight and Sunday morning ministry for Launch kids, include a group devotion and prayer in your weeknight event. Your weeknight events can also include group games and snacks and be interspersed with Parent Nights, presentations by special guests, group projects (such as making cookies or gift packs for people in the community), holiday celebrations, and missional service.

Use purchased curricula in your Sunday morning sessions. Look for curriculum lessons written especially for preteens that fit into the Hook/Book/Look/Took teaching outline.

Hook. Begin with a question, illustration, or personal experience from your own or someone else's life that connects the biblical truth with a preteen need.

Book. Have Launch kids find each week's passage of Scripture in the Bible and follow along as they take turns reading it aloud. If possible, have copies of an easier-to-read children's version of the Bible available for the kids to use. Having everyone read from this same version will clear up a lot of confusion.

Look. Prepare thought-provoking questions that help the kids respond to the passage as they read it. Leave lots of time and space for verbal input from the kids throughout the lesson.

Ongoing discussion not only helps them process the lesson; it also helps channel their tendency to engage in side conversations with each other. Include questions like "What do you think God is saying to us in these verses? How do you feel about that? How can what God is saying help or change us?"

Whenever the passage is a story that features Jesus, ask questions that help the kids see Jesus in the story. Encourage them to use their imaginations to be there with Him.

Use a variety of discussion prompters from week to week:

- Neighbour nudging. For example, they can turn to a friend and tell their friend what they notice about Jesus in the story, and then ask their friend what they notice about Him.
- Interviews. For example, have one or two preteens pretend to be characters in the story. Interview each character about their experience with Jesus.
- Visual reflections. For example, show the kids an artist's portrayal of the story. Ask, "If you were in the boat with Jesus and the disciples, where would you be in the picture?"
- Artistic expressions. For example, they can draw a picture to show what they think God wants us to learn from this story. Or they can use pipe cleaners to sculpt an emoji that shows how this story makes them feel.
- Connect with music. For example, play a song that describes a need or emotion Jesus had or cared about in the story.

Gather all the pencils, paper, and other items you and the kids will need for these learning activities before the session starts. Interrupting the Bible study unnecessarily makes it hard for the kids to stay focussed.

Preteens, and all of us, are surrounded by people who think God only expects us to be nice and pursue our own happiness. Lead the kids into Scripture that helps them perceive a true image of God and holiness. Help them see that some attitudes and actions are right, and others are wrong. Point out ways in which even the best Bible characters fell short of God's holiness.

Took. Encourage the kids to share personal stories about the ways God is working in their lives. Naming, and hearing their friends name, the most important thing God showed them in a passage can help move truth from their heads to their hearts.

Invite the kids to pray with you about these specific takeaways. Encourage them to talk with Jesus directly, telling Him honestly how they feel and asking Him for His help.

Forging the Trail

When we started the Trail at the West End Baptist Church, we introduced it in the Sunday morning worship service and then celebrated it with a tailgate party that afternoon. We invited the congregation to pack a picnic lunch and bring it along to a big parking lot near one of the city's beautiful ponds.

As people arrived, we sent them out onto the walking trail that circled the pond. Volunteers were stationed at various points along the trail to explain the different sections of our Trail and pass out appropriate treats.

The event ended with a big intergenerational picnic back in the parking lot. A symbolic hike and barbecued hot dogs are simple things, but they were a fun way to mark the start of something new.

FORGING OR BUILDING THE TRAIL IN A CHURCH IS A LONG-TERM project. But don't discount it for this reason. Keep in mind that every advance with the Trail, no matter how small, strengthens your children's ministry.

Imagine forging the Trail in your church the way the Trans Canada hiking/biking trail was built on our old railway beds, layer by layer and one section at a time. It took a few years to complete the Trans Canada Trail and it may take a few years to build all the sections of your children's ministry Trail.

Even after the entire Trail has been built, it will need constant grooming and annual repairs. Vision fades and needs to be recast. Human nature kicks in and we drift from intentionality toward what is easiest. Volunteers leave. There are volunteer gaps. Then new volunteers come and have to be taught the ways of the Trail.

We outgrow spaces. The budget changes. Familiar curricula and other published resources are discontinued. New families and children with different needs challenge our proven strategies.

Expect these changes. Aim for excellence but expect the forging of the Trail to be an ongoing effort.

When it comes to the Trail, the greatest challenge may be knowing where and how to begin. Whether we're starting a new children's ministry or transforming an already existing one, the big question is "Where do we start?"

Consider starting with the section of the Trail that has the greatest number of children or the greatest potential number of children. If the largest number of children in your church are in early elementary school, between five and eight years of age, you may want to start with Discover. Or if children this age are plentiful in your neighbourhood but not in your church, consider starting a ministry with this age group wherever they already are. Is your local community centre or daycare open to Bible learning activities run by church volunteers? Could you begin to build the Discover section of the Trail with a park ministry or day camp?

Forging the Launch section of the Trail requires a lot of creative effort and energy, but if we're providing a rich spiritual formation experience for preteens, they will be the quickest to grow their group by inviting friends. Younger children are more apt to join when parents invite parents, but Launch kids are good at inviting peers to join them in something they enjoy. Launch kids can also be the key to reaching whole families. They often have younger and older siblings.

If an entire age group of children or teens is missing in your church, you may want to start building the Trail with the section just before that age group. For example, a vibrant Launch ministry can eventually evolve into a dynamic youth ministry.

Plan to make a fresh investment in the Welcome section of the Trail each time a baby is born. Every baby shower and every Ceremony of Promise and Blessing helps build the Welcome section of the Trail.

Whenever you're ready to start a new section of the Trail, begin by helping the volunteers who work in that section grasp age-appropriate spiritual goals and concepts. Show them how to use the curriculum to design lesson plans that help the children make these spiritual goals and concepts part of their lives. Meet with volunteers regularly to help them evaluate their ministry against Trail goals. Build the Trail one volunteer, one ministry team, and one section at a time.

Safety on the Trail

I can't really remember why they asked me to be at camp that week. I wasn't a counsellor. I think they wanted me to be an older adult presence, kind of like a chaplain.

It sounded like a great idea, but when I got there I felt like a fish out of water. Shy and uncertain of my role, I didn't initiate connections with the children the way I should have. Miserable, I watched as the children swarmed their teenaged counsellors.

Then one little girl asked if she could talk with me. Secretly thrilled, I got up and walked away from the group with her. We were some distance away from the others before I realized my mistake. This child clearly wanted adult attention, so I steered her back toward the others where I could give it to her safely, in plain view of everyone else.

IN TODAY'S TROUBLED WORLD, A WORLD MADE EVEN MORE WORRISOME with constantly expanding media coverage, parents care more about their child's safety than ever before. In fact, the lack of carefully planned and implemented protection for all minors in our children and youth ministries is often a dealbreaker for parents when it comes to visiting and/or returning to a church. Parents must feel confident that their children are safe and receiving good care before they can relax and engage in worship and other spiritually formative experiences.

But this is just one reason why every section of the Trail must be built within the sturdy guardrails of a sound child protection plan or policy.[26]

A well planned and consistently implemented child protection plan plays a vital role in keeping the children in our care safe from sexual abuse and other dangers. It also helps protect church volunteers from false accusations.

And even though our primary goal and concern is to reduce the risk of danger for minors and volunteers, a sound child protection policy will also reduce risk for your church. If an incident occurs in one of your ministries, the church's reputation could be ruined, and the church could be sued for millions of dollars.[27] The physical, emotional, and spiritual damage done to a child is devastating, and so is the damage done to a local church, all churches, and the reputation of Christ.[28]

Too often, churches form a committee that writes a protection policy and then sets the document aside, leaving the children's ministry to operate apart from it. Sometimes the protection policy is written too elaborately to be clearly understood. Or it is so extensive that it's impractical to implement.

It's helpful to divide the protection policy into three main sections:

- Screening volunteers.
- Supervising volunteers.
- Reporting allegations.

Essential points for supervision should include:

---

26 See Appendix 3: Sample Child Protection Policy.
27 Consult your church's insurance company for advice regarding your policy.
28 I have learned much of this from the "Reducing the Risk" child protection training manual and teaching DVDs produced by *Christianity Today*. This is an excellent resource.

Safety on the Trail

- Never be alone with a child.
- Use only appropriate touch.
- Insist that children ask permission before leaving the group.

Children's ministry volunteers must work together to hold one another accountable for the rules and help each other comply with them.

Recruiting Trailblazers

It was an unusual place for me to start and I can't remember how I got onto it. It must have been a God-thing. But one day I went to some of our church's dads with preteens and asked if they would help lead a Friday night Launch group.

These dads were amazing. They shared devotional thoughts and led in prayer. One dad even wrote a prayer just for our Launch kids! The dads loved the same sports and high-energy games as the kids and built a terrific rapport with them.

A couple of moms helped out, too, and they were great with snacks and organizing events. But the dads brought extra layers of effectiveness to our Launch ministry. They laughed and teased and kept us from taking ourselves too seriously. They were wonderful role models for the kids, some of whom were being raised by single moms. They even loaded up their cars with their own kids' friends and brought them along to Launch every week.

The group kept growing.

Reflecting on it now, I marvel over the fact that the dads weren't only ideal leaders for Launch; being involved in Launch also helped them. It gave them a consistent opportunity to engage with their own preteen children… and it gave them an opportunity to hang out with other dads.

RECRUITING THE RIGHT PEOPLE TO PROVIDE SPIRITUAL NURTURE FOR children in the church begins with an exciting, purposeful, and well-articulated vision. Before people can become interested in getting involved, they need to catch a glimpse of what we aim to accomplish.

People value their time at least as much as their money, so volunteers don't want to simply "do a job." They want to know that their contribution makes a Kingdom difference. Be encouraged! As soon as even just one or two people find their God-crafted niche in the plan, God's Spirit releases an exciting momentum that catches others up in the vision.

Some volunteers will themselves be gifted visionaries and do their best work if they can imagine their own strategies for getting the job done. Other volunteers may want to be given a strategy to follow and then released to make it happen. Recruited teams should be allowed to think for themselves as much as possible. When they do, they own their work, invest more in it, and find it increasingly satisfying. Volunteers who bring their own expertise and creativity to the task raise the effectiveness of the ministry to whole new levels.

Build Teams

Another important part of the recruiting process is to build volunteer teams instead of overwhelming one person with many different tasks.

For example, each section of the Trail needs effective leaders, but a volunteer who may not be comfortable working directly with the children may be willing to join the team as an administrative director. This job can include scheduling volunteers, ordering curricula, registering the children, etc. Other volunteers may prefer to work as helpers who focus on nurturing loving relationships with the children as they guide their learning and behaviour. Still others may join the team as an audio/visual director, a music leader, a storyteller, etc.

Ideally, leaders who work with children will have a healthy degree of spiritual maturity, but not everyone on the team must be at the same level. Serving in God-appointed ways can itself nurture our spiritual growth. Watch for opportunities to help your volunteers take the next step in their own spiritual development.

God has designed the church to be most effective when individuals are fitting their spiritual passions and gifts together with the spiritual passions and gifts of others (1 Corinthians 12:12–20, Ephesians 4:11–13). Every children's ministry team needs a variety of gifts and abilities. And teams that brainstorm, pray, and argue every side of every issue together will be stronger, smarter, more fun, and a whole lot more effective than any one person trying to accomplish something on their own.

God works through ministry teams to nurture the children, but He also uses teamwork to accomplish spiritual formation in the lives of team members. Working with others shows us our need for God's help to better understand and appreciate ourselves and others.

Pray. As you work to fit the right person onto the team, one volunteer and one task at a time, ask God to show you who is the best person for each job. Pray for that person to be open. Always approach the person who seems best for the job first, even if it seems like they have a good reason to say no. Trust God to overcome obstacles so His will can be done.

It pays to go slowly and build the team well right from the start. Bathe the entire process in prayer and enjoy the challenge! It's a lot like fitting together the pieces of a jigsaw puzzle, one right fit at a time.

Be up close and personal. It's best to approach people first in person. But when circumstances won't allow a face-to-face interview, a computer or phone call can serve as a reasonable alternative.

Rarely should people be asked to commit to an important ministry in an email or text. An exception would be recruiting for tasks that require a lot of people to give little effort and only a small amount of time. For example, blitzing the neighbourhood with promo flyers for a kids' event.

Craft job descriptions. When you approach a person, give them a clear description of the job to be done, what they will need to do it and why, how much time it will take, and who will be working with them. Never assume that people automatically know and understand these things.

The right person will be drawn to a manageable challenge, so be careful not to downplay the role. Be honest about parts of the job that are "still under construction," because the right person may be able to help with these.

Have clear systems of accountability and support in place. Tell the volunteer who will provide the direction, support, and resources they need. Also, be honest about additional expectations, such as how often they will be expected to meet with the rest of the team.

Ask the volunteer to commit for a reasonable length of time and then meet with you again to evaluate their experience. Assure them that at that meeting they can either recommit to or be released from the task.

Follow up. After you've presented a clear job description, ask the volunteer to pray about the opportunity for a few days. Encourage them to find out from God if it's what He is calling them to do. It's important that they accept the job because they believe it's what God wants them to do and not just because they were asked. Trust God to make His will known to the volunteer as they pray. Pray along with them.

Check back with the volunteer for their decision when you said you would, usually no longer than a week or two. If they say no, thank them for giving it prayerful consideration. It's okay to express your disappointment, but don't make them feel guilty. Accept by faith that they have prayed about this and heard from the Lord.

Trust God to be in the process and to lead you to the right person. Expect the recruitment process to be labour-intensive, especially when you're building a new team. Pray, contact, and then pray and contact again. Don't give up! The thrill of watching the right team players take a ministry to a whole new level is well worth the effort!

Bank awareness. Recruiting trailblazers is a perpetual process of getting to know people. Have ongoing conversations and even intentional interviews with people to help them be increasingly aware of the unique way God has designed them for His specific purposes. Affirm people by sincerely telling them why you think they will be good at a certain task or in a particular role.

Experimentation is an important part of the self-discovery process, so let people try children's ministry. If it isn't a good fit for them, help them find a mission or ministry that is. Experimentation is especially important for youth and young adults. One of the developmental tasks for people in their stage of life is to discover their passion and abilities; experimenting with different ministry opportunities helps them with this.

As important as it is to include self-discovery exercises and experiment with various types of ministry, the key to growing self-awareness is getting to know God better. God helps us know ourselves and our calling as we pursue a deepening relationship with Him.

Stay with the team. It may be surprising to realize that the recruitment process isn't finished when a volunteer says yes and accepts the job. At that point, recruitment transitions into the twin tasks of supervision and affirmation.

Providing effective supervision includes learning to walk the tightrope between maintaining too much control over volunteers and completely abandoning them. We will have to arrive at the right tension for each volunteer since some will want and deserve considerable independence right out of the gate while others will need plenty of support and encouragement to get started.

When volunteers want to work independently, we may have to hold them accountable for the church's bigger vision. Strong and gifted leaders can easily swerve off and start ministries that work at cross-purposes with the church's main vision and mission. Invest time and energy, at least initially, showing these volunteers that the ministry you have recruited them to do is an exciting, worthwhile part of a bigger enterprise.

Volunteers who are stepping into a new ministry experience may need apprenticing. Apprenticing is essentially on-the-job training and is best done as a four-step process:

- I do the job and you watch me.
- I do the job and you help me.
- You do the job and I help you.
- You do the job and I watch you.

Apprenticing is a graduated way to release control and empower a volunteer with new responsibility.

Navigating the right tension with each volunteer means consistently paying attention. Volunteers will love their work if we give them enough responsibility to challenge them and enough freedom to inspire them, but they will quickly become discouraged if we withhold resources and support and/or fail to communicate as often and clearly as we should. It's a bit like raising kids to become mature adults, gradually and appropriately releasing control but continuing to be a caring, encouraging presence in their lives no matter what.

Work with the team. Regular contact with children's ministry volunteers can include checking in with a quick email, text, or Sunday morning "How's it going?" But it should also include bringing the team together. Ideally, team meetings should happen as early as possible in the fall, as early as possible in January, and/or whenever new initiatives are introduced.

Every time the team meets, use Trail goals to help volunteers evaluate their ministry. Give each volunteer a printed evaluation form (see the sample below) and ask them to circle the number that best represents their ministry's current effectiveness with each goal.

When volunteers have finished rating each goal, ask them to explain why they rated each one as they did. Brainstorm ways to become more effective, especially with the goals that got the lowest ratings. For example, if "Church Is a Family for My Family" got a low rating, have volunteers commit to engaging parents in more friendly conversation when they drop off and pick up their children.

Plan to include a brief training segment each time the team meets. Use a short video to stimulate discussion on a particular topic, invite a guest to share an idea they are using in their children's ministry, recruit a panel to present their perspectives on an issue, or read and discuss a brief article. Include a review of your church's child protection policy. Identify aspects of the protection plan that need to be strengthened in your part of the Trail and commit to these improvements.

Team meetings can also include spiritual nurture for volunteers and give them a sense of community they may not otherwise have. Encourage volunteers to talk about the rewards and blessings they are experiencing. Infuse meetings with gratitude to God for all He is doing and with honest expressions of appreciation for your volunteers. Brighten these times together with meaningful and creative ways to acknowledge accomplished goals and celebrate wins.

Most volunteers will balk at having to give more of their time to meetings. Piggyback team meetings with other events most team members will be attending. Keep your sessions meaningful and no longer than an hour and a half.

Finally, persevere. Trust God and work with whoever shows up!

Sample Ministry Evaluation Form

This sample form lists Welcome goals, but you can substitute Wonder, Discover, or Launch goals for each of these specific ministries.

Circle the number that best represents our current effectiveness with each Welcome goal.
1 represents the least effective, 5 represents the most effective.

God Made Me:	1	2	3	4	5
Jesus Loves Me:	1	2	3	4	5
Church Is a Happy Place to Be:	1	2	3	4	5
Church Is a Family for My Family:	1	2	3	4	5

Parents on the Trail

When our children were young, Fridays were family night at our house. At the risk of leaving you feeling exhausted and/or having you think we were crazy, I'll tell you we had magic shows, talent shows, and pretend-trips to other countries.

One night we draped blankets over the backs of the dining room chairs and slept in a "tent" on the living room floor. That is, the children and I did. My husband, ordinarily a very good sport, drew the line at sleeping on the floor when there was a perfectly good bed just down the hall.

The children and I finally gave up on him, cozied into our sleeping bags, and were enjoying a bedtime story by flashlight when we were startled by a bump outside the "tent."

It's putting it mildly to say we were startled! The children pushed so close to me that I was sure they could hear my heart thumping.

Then we heard a gruff voice say, "This is Ranger Rick. All lights must be turned off!"

Everything erupted into screams of terror, incredulity, and then laughing relief when we realized that Ranger Rick, otherwise known as Dad, hadn't wanted to miss the fun after all.

These family nights were a lot of work and took considerable energy. Other things didn't get done. My husband and I do have parenting regrets, but taking time to play with our children isn't one of them. We saw it as investing... in the children, in our relationship with them, in our own need to relax and play, and in our bank of family memories.

As I mentioned earlier, the book I read about strengthening children's ministry that most gripped and compelled me was *Transforming Children into Spiritual Champions* by George Barna. He wrote, "The role of the church in the spiritual formation of a child is crucial, but a child's family is central."[29] His research shows that of all the things that influence a person's spirituality, their parents are among the most influential. This is especially true during the early, formative years.[30]

Just about the time God put the George Barna book in my hands, He started a movement in churches in the U.S. called the Deuteronomy 6 (D6) movement. This was a huge shift back to seeing the home as the powerhouse of spiritual formation in children.

Soon God called Mark Holman, author of *Faith Begins at Home*;[31] Brain Haynes, author of *Shift*; Reggie Joiner, author of *Think Orange*; and other teachers and authors to lead us onto this new/old frontier.

I call it a new/old frontier because seeing the home as the powerhouse of spiritual formation in children takes us back to what God instituted in Jewish culture thousands of years ago. His instructions regarding the centrality of parenting in spiritual formation is clearly recorded in Deuteronomy 6:4–9. This passage popped out at all of us who were wrestling for greater effectiveness in the spiritual formation of children during the early years of the new millennium.

In these verses, God instructs parents to be their children's primary teachers of faith and godly obedience and to do this naturally as they live out the rhythms of daily life.

---

29 Barna, *Transforming Children in Spiritual Champions*, 14.
30 Ibid., 58.
31 Mark Holman, *Faith Begins at Home: The Family Makeover with Christ at the Center* (Ventura, CA: Regal Books, 2005).

Hear, O Israel: The Lord our God, the Lord is one. Love the Lord your God with all your heart and with all your soul and with all your strength. These commandments that I give you today are to be on your hearts. Impress them on your children. Talk about them when you sit at home and when you walk along the road, when you lie down and when you get up. Tie them as symbols on your hands and bind them on your foreheads. Write them on the doorframes of your houses and on your gates.

—Deuteronomy 6:4–9

These words are repeated with a promise in Deuteronomy 11:18–21:

Fix these words of mine in your hearts and minds; tie them as symbols on your hands and bind them on your foreheads. Teach them to your children, talking about them when you sit at home and when you walk along the road, when you lie down and when you get up. Write them on the doorframes of your houses and on your gates, so that your days and the days of your children may be many in the land the Lord swore to give your ancestors, as many as the days that the heavens are above the earth.

The principle of parents passing faith on to their children is also referred to in other scriptures:

My people, hear my teaching; listen to the words of my mouth. I will open my mouth with a parable; I will utter hidden things, things from of old—things we have heard and known, things our ancestors have told us. We will not hide them from their descendants; we will tell the next generation the praiseworthy deeds of the Lord, his power, and the wonders he has done. He decreed statutes for Jacob and established the law in Israel, which he commanded

> our ancestors to teach their children, so the next generation would know them, even the children yet to be born, and they in turn would tell their children. Then they would put their trust in God and would not forget his deeds but would keep his commands.
> —Psalm 78:1–7

> Fathers, do not exasperate your children; instead, bring them up in the training and instruction of the Lord.
> —Ephesians 6:4

Other biblical passages that speak in more general terms of one generation passing their faith in God along to the next include Psalm 71:17–18, Psalm 89:1, and Psalm 145:3–7.

Natural Rhythms

Going back to Deuteronomy 6, and particularly to the part about sharing our faith with our children as we live out the natural rhythms of daily life, we read,

> These commandments that I give you today are to be on your hearts. Impress them on your children. Talk about them when you sit at home and when you walk along the road, when you lie down and when you get up.
> —Deuteronomy 6:6–7

Reggie Joiner suggests that the outline God gives us in Deuteronomy 6:7 is timeless and fits the natural routine of family life in any culture. Generally speaking, all people groups since the beginning of time have gotten up with the sun, moved around in the day, shared a meal, and slept through the night. Deuteronomy 6 provides lots of opportunity for spiritual nourishment that's intentional, informal, intimate, and inspirational.[32]

The phrase *"when you sit at home"* could refer to a mealtime and an intentional time of focussing on a verse or story from the Bible followed by a time of talking about it. The phrase *"when you walk along the road"* could refer to an informal time spent with your kids in the car, singing praise songs, and/or chatting with them about God and His perspective on things. The phrase *"when you lie down"* could refer to an intimate time of sharing with God and with one another at bedtime. The phrase *"when you get up"* could refer to an opportunity to inspire your kids to see the day ahead as a gift from God and ask for His help with it.

When our children were growing up, I wouldn't let them leave for school until I had prayed a blessing over them. Some days we'd be running late, with me driving them to school, battling traffic, and praying with my eyes open. It was messy, but I think what made it holy was quite simply this: we knew it was important.

The Critical Role Parents Play in Spiritual Formation

The idea that parents play a critical role in the spiritual formation of their children is supported by a number of principles. In addition to Larry Richards's seven principles for effective role-modelling,[33] consider the following:

- As we have seen from God's Word, spirituality is best taught/caught in the normal rhythms of daily life.
- As we have already learned from George Barna, parents have the greatest influence on their children, for better or worse. This is especially true during the

---

32 Joiner, *Think Orange*, 66.
33 See Appendix 4: Larry Richard's Seven Principles for Effective Role-Modelling

early, formative years.[34] Parents have a natural authority in their child's life and children automatically look to their example.

- Parents have time on their side. A child who goes to church every week averages forty hours with church teachers and leaders per year, time that's often watered down by interruptions, managing group behaviour, etc. Pre-COVID, attending church regularly for a lot of families meant being there every second week, so think an average of twenty hours per year in church. That number has been reduced even further by the pandemic. But the child we're tracking still averages three thousand hours per year with their parent(s).[35]
- Parents are not only with their children more, they're also with their children longer. Church leaders come and go, but parents are usually connected to their children for a lifetime. As George Barna points out, "Spiritual development is a lifelong, continual process."[36] Parents are the people God has put in place to look after it.
- Because parents live everyday life with their children, they can demonstrate and explain the practical application of God's Word as life unfolds for the child. Church teachers rely heavily, although not always exclusively, on simulated applications. Parents are also in a better position to see their children's attitudes and behaviours, which indicate whether or not they're absorbing a spiritual concept. And they can hold their

---

34 Barna, *Transforming Children into Spiritual Champions*, 58.
35 Joiner, *Think Orange*, 87–88.
36 Barna, *Transforming Children into Spiritual Champions*, 82.

children accountable for spiritual disciplines, such as limited screentime.

Partners on the Trail

I tried lots of ways to bring parents together for coaching, encouragement, and mutual support along the Trail. We hosted several after-church luncheons and discussions. I thought inviting a panel of older parents to share their wisdom was especially brilliant.

But my all-time favourite was a spaghetti super we organized for parents and their young children on Valentine's Day. We pulled a few highchairs up to the tables, agreed that spaghetti was the messiest meal we could have served, and then sent the children off to play with the teenagers we had hired to babysit.

There were red and pink hearts everywhere. We played some sort of icebreaker with hearts and tried to get to the "heart" of parenting with some discussion starters.

If I could do it over again, I would have started with more heart-to-heart talks with individual parents—listening to their struggles and joys, and asking them directly how the church could be a bigger help to them.

I'm ashamed to admit that my arrogance (I thought I knew what they needed) and insecurities (I was afraid they would reject my ideas) kept our ministries with parents from being as effective as they could have been. My heart was in the right place, but I wish it had been much more open.

PARENTS PLAY A CENTRAL ROLE IN THE SPIRITUAL FORMATION OF THEIR children, but ideally parents and the church link up along the Trail to form a partnership. There are many ways in which the church can contribute to this partnership. The church can lead both children and their parents into the light of God's Word, which reveals God and God's perspective on life. This is called a biblical worldview.

We read in the Bible, *"Your word is a lamp for my feet, a light on my path... The unfolding of your words gives light; it gives understanding to the simple"* (Psalm 119:105, 130). The church provides this scriptural light in the teaching offered to both children and parents. Parents need to be growing spiritually in order to help their children grow.

The church can help hold people accountable for the practice of personal disciplines (daily time alone with the Lord, personal Bible reading, etc.) and provide opportunities for parents and their children to practice corporate disciplines (worship, community, etc.). The spiritual disciplines we develop play a crucial role in our spiritual formation. They open places in space and time where we can experience God's presence.

The church can provide role models who teach the same values a child's parents teach. In *Think Orange*, author Reggie Joiner says, "Two combined influences make a much greater influence than just two influences."[37]

For example, if parents and the church teach the same biblical principle each week, this has the potential to make a much greater impact on the child than if, in the same week, parents teach one biblical truth and the church another. In a more general way, hearing other voices that are saying the same things as one's parents is especially important as children reach preadolescence and adolescence.

The church can provide peer friendships with other children and youth who are also being raised according to a biblical worldview.

Additionally, the church can function as a faith community that demonstrates, even if imperfectly, biblical values in its relationships with one another.

---

37 Joiner, *Think Orange*, 23.

The church can also provide intergenerational events where parents and children can enjoy and strengthen relationships with people of all ages. It has been said that it takes a family to raise a child, but a good community sure helps.

The church can provide teaching on family life from a biblical perspective to strengthen families. For example, marriage enrichment, financial management, etc.

The church can provide support systems for parents who are committed to the task of spiritually nurturing their children. For example, small groups for parents, mentors for parents, etc.

The church can provide ongoing practical help for parents who want to parent their children God's way. For example, the church can suggest one simple thing each week that parents can do to become increasingly intentional with their parenting.

Why It's Important for the Church to Help Parents

Many parents want help with their parenting. They're saying, "Give me a plan for the spiritual nurture of my child. Tell me what to say. Show me what to do."[38]

Many of today's parents have not had good parental examples. Left to ourselves, we tend to parent the way we were parented.

Also, many parents think that only the church can provide the spiritual nurture their children need. So they're happy to bring their children to church or even just drop them off. Spiritual nurture at home can be a foreign concept to parents who have never seen it modelled.

The church has contributed to the problem. Several decades ago, we staffed our churches with Christian education professionals (I was one of them) and marketed all kinds of Christian education

---

38 Ibid., 90.

programs, implying, I think, that these programs would be all the spiritual help a child would need.

There is training for parents available in our broader community, but only the church can help parents with spiritual nurture. As Barna points out, every other aspect of who we are can only be healthy if we get the spiritual component right.[39] Our self-image, character development, relationships with others, morality, and choices will be healthier and more wholesome when they are aligned with a correct understanding of God and the way He views us and life itself.

Because our society has moved away from the centrality of God and the church at the heart of our communities, many churchgoing believers no longer have a clear biblical worldview. The influences of the media and consumerism have infiltrated our thinking to the extent that many parents don't even recognize the difference between God's perspective and the world's perspective on various issues. How can they teach their children the difference if they don't see it?

The church must shine the light of God's Word to show parents the contrast between the world's thinking and God's thinking. For example, many of today's parents will tell you that their main parenting goal is to raise their kids to be happy. But when that's your perceived parenting goal, it makes disciplining your children very difficult.

Here's another example. The world tells kids that they only have value if they have beauty, brains, and bucks. God tells them they have value because He made them, loves them enough to die for them, and designed them to fulfill His purposes in the world.

Writer Linda V. Callahan gives us this challenge: "Parents need to do something they have never been required to do before

---

39 Barna, *Transforming Children into Spiritual Champions*, 28–29.

perhaps at any time in history: deliberately and consciously counter many of the dominant messages of our own culture."[40]

---

40 Linda V. Callahan, "Turning Down the Noise: Reading and the Development of Spirituality in Children," *Nurturing Children's Spirituality: Christian Perspectives and Best Practices*, Holly Catterton Allen, ed. (Eugene, OR: Cascade Books, 2008), 173.

Building the Partnership

Our children were teenagers when I got ordained. Before going ahead with it, I talked with them. One of them said, "Well, Mom, we're already PKs"—that's pastor's kids, for the uninitiated—"so how much worse can it get?"

It was true, I had a lot of expectations for them.

Thankfully, their father was much wiser.

"Let's not raise our children to be PKs," he said when they were born. "Let's raise them to be followers of Jesus."

The test came when they both landed parts in the school play. Rehearsals were Sunday mornings and they asked to be excused from church for several weeks so they could keep their commitment to the play.

I panicked.

Oh no, I thought, We can't let them miss church! If they aren't in church, what will people think?

I had already judged and condemned us as both parents and pastors, but I don't think my husband ever feared for his job or reputation. He calmly asked the kids why it was important for them to be in church on Sunday mornings. They had good answers. (I may have helped a little.)

"What are your options?" he asked them.

"We have to miss one or the other," they said.

But then we brainstormed beyond the obvious.

"You could go to Sunday evening worship with some of your Salvation Army friends," their dad suggested.

This calmed me down a little. They wouldn't be at our church, but they would be at church.

"Or you could explain to your teachers that you have a previous commitment on Sunday mornings, and you'll be a little late for rehearsals," their dad continued. "Think and pray about it. Mom and I will support whatever you decide to do."

They chose the last option.

Their teachers were impressed. Their father wasn't surprised. And I lived to tell you that even people who write about parenting worry about their parenting and being judged for it.

NO MATTER HOW READY, EAGER, AND EVEN COMMITTED WE ARE TO partner with parents in the spiritual nurture of their children, our greatest challenge may be finding effective ways to engage parents in the partnership. It will help to understand some reasons parents tend to resist parent training opportunities.

Parents often feel that they are too busy, that they have no time to learn God's way of parenting. We will have to encourage parents to be intentional with their parenting.

Jeff Foxworthy put it this way:

> Being a good parent is hard, and in the short term there is not a lot of glory attached to it. But you can't coast through it. Good parenting is intentional. Anybody can have a child. Being a good parent takes work and prayer... A hundred years from now, your great-grandchildren probably won't even know your name. No one will care about what awards you won or how much money you made. The only thing that will matter is what kind of children you left behind and their influence on subsequent generations.[41]

---

[41] Reggie Joiner and Carey Nieuwhof, *Parenting Beyond Your Capacity: Connect Your Family to a Wider Community* (Colorado Springs, CO: David C. Cook, 2010), 13–14. Quoting Jeff Foxworthy, who wrote the book's foreword.

We may have to help parents rethink their priorities so they can be intentional and at the same time assure them that being intentional doesn't have to be overwhelming.

Some parents feel that learning to parent God's way isn't necessary. They think, *My parents didn't get any training and I turned out okay.* We will have to help parents who didn't experience spiritual nurture as a child catch a vision for it.

Many parents aren't yet Christians and don't see the need for a spiritual component in their parenting. But these same parents are apt to take parenting itself seriously. Invite them to parenting events, and set every parenting event in a relaxed environment. Include elements of fun and teamwork. Let God speak to seekers through the honesty, friendship, and viewpoints of other parents. Never force parents to speak—but when they do, respect their opinions and affirm whatever you can in what they say.

The most effective way to engage parents who aren't yet Christians is to involve their children in the event you want the parents to attend. If children are loving your Trail ministries, they will encourage their parents to come with them whenever they can, especially if the child has been asked to do something at the event.

Most if not all parents, perhaps even more Christian than non-Christian parents, feel inadequate and guilty about their parenting. Add to that a fear that the church will judge them for poor parenting. Strangers to the church and even pastors, perhaps especially pastors, struggle with this fear. The fear can cause us to project impossible and graceless expectations on ourselves and on our children.

We can encourage other parents to relax by learning to accept the imperfections in ourselves, in our own parenting, and in our own children the way God does. Instead of setting too-high expectations, we can help other parents move further into God's grace and way of parenting one small step at a time. We can encourage one another to focus on God's compassionate understanding of our human weaknesses and lean into Him for help with them.

Christian parents may feel defeated by the complexities of modern life and the strength of distorting views in schools, the media, and our overall culture. Help parents understand that if we don't present the Christian alternative, our children will never realize it's an alternative. Not presenting the Christian worldview increases the likelihood of them adhering to another.

Many parents think, *I'm no expert on Christianity. I'm not doing so well in my own walk with the Lord.* Parents don't need to be experts on spiritual issues, nor do they need to excel spiritually. All parents need in order to be spiritually authentic and effective is to be honest and willing to grow.

Parents also think, *I'm afraid I'll say something wrong and mess up my kids.* God is bigger than our mistakes. In fact, He's in the business of redeeming them. Mistakes are inevitable. It's what we do with our mistakes that matters.

More wise words from Jeff Foxworthy: "You will make plenty of mistakes [as a parent] and that's okay. Mistakes are often opportunities to show your children, not only your fragile humanity, but also the way you respond to failure."[42]

A parent already has so much responsibility that adding the spiritual dimension can feel overwhelming. But as author John Trent says, "Training our children spiritually is not rocket science."[43] We simply take things at our child's pace… one bite size piece at a time.

Parents worry, *What if I do all this and my child still doesn't choose to believe?* There are no guarantees, but we have the opportunity to give our parenting to God as an offering of our love for Him, and as an offering of love for our child, trusting God with our intentionality.

---

42 Ibid., 14.
43 John Trent and Jane Vogel, *Faith Launch: A Simple Plan to Ignite Your Child's Love for Jesus* (Carol Stream, IL: Tyndale House, 2008), 6.

Good News!

I first realized the possibility of an effective partnership between today's parents and the church when I read an article that Rick Chromey, founder and director of Manna! Educational Services International, wrote about millennials. According to that article, today's parents may be more open to a partnership with the church than previous generations. Can we draw on some of the following generalities to connect with them?

- Today's parents feel overwhelmed by the amount of parenting information that is available. They tend to feel that their parenting is being judged by other parents because of relational pressure on social media. They need to be reassured that they're doing a good job and that we are all in this together.
- They want to make a difference in the world. They like to do things with positive, practical outcomes: gardening, food banks, yard work for a senior, or serving the poor and homeless. They aren't interested in programs for programming's sake.
- They are collaborative and enjoy teamwork.
- Technology is their world. They want tech communication that is clear and quick.
- They are drawn to authenticity, not authority. They want to learn from people who are honest, transparent, and non-judgmental.
- They aren't afraid to ask for help. They want us to point them to the right resources and provide practical suggestions.
- They want whatever works. It doesn't matter if it's a new idea or age-old wisdom.

- They want what's best for their families. They delight in their children and are willing to follow them. So win the hearts of their children and let their children lead them!

Digital Expressions of the Trail

During the pandemic, I took a peek at some online ministries for kids. Churches were doing an amazing job, being resilient, innovative, creative, and resourceful. All these words came to mind as I watched children's pastors and volunteers do something they had never done before.

I found out that one church prepared and delivered lesson kits to every child's home each week. It was expensive and time-consuming, but it meant that every child had colouring pictures, puzzles, playdough, pipe cleaners, and whatever else they needed for every learning activity. Others featured puppets or fun, mascot-like characters. Still others kept us interested with ongoing projects. On one site, I watched a bean plant grow from week to week! Some online kids' ministries even had parents prerecord their children's responses to open-ended questions and presented these as part of the lesson.

But I have to say, in a show of nepotism, that the prize goes to the church where my niece directs the children's ministries. Parents brought their children to an outdoor location and dressed them in costumes. Then, with amazing technology—and, I'm sure, careful regard for social distancing—the children enacted a Bible story.

And so it was that the children themselves presented the online lesson that week.

Fun fact: it was Christmas and the children playacted the birth of Jesus. COVID fact: they did it outdoors. Canadian fact: it might be harder to play-act the birth of Jesus at Christmas outdoors here in Canada; my niece's church is in Australia. Digital fact: isn't it amazing that even though she's so far away, I could see what she was doing with just a couple of clicks on the computer?

Children On the Trail

DURING THE COVID-19 PANDEMIC, CHURCHES EVERYWHERE BEGAN TO do children's ministry online.

Two years later, we're still experimenting with digital ministries. Most churches are now developing a hybrid or mixed approach: a return to real-time gatherings combined with digital postings.

Although we would all most likely agree that being in the same physical space is best when it comes to teaching children, digital expressions of the Trail can:

- reach children who aren't in church.
- engage parents in their child's spiritual formation.
- show parents what the church has to offer and engage them in ongoing conversations.
- provide virtual one-on-one and small group experiences.

Reach children who aren't in church. Age-appropriate children's sessions that can be accessed online are fast becoming a missional extension of the church. If your church produces its own sessions, work with the Hook/Book/Look/Took outline you would use to design a Discover lesson.

But keep it simple! Look for a simple, sustainable pattern and use simple "I wonder…" conversation starters. Engage children from your church in the presentations. Let them playact the Bible story, respond to open-ended questions, and/or participate in other meaningful but creative ways.

If producing your own weekly virtual lessons for children is an unrealistic goal for your church, consider using professionally produced videos. Connect these to online forums that allow kids to check in and talk about what they're learning.

Engage parents in their child's spiritual formation. There are several different options for using digital expressions of the Trail to engage parents in their children's spiritual formation.

Number one, encourage parents to watch online lessons with their children and use "I wonder…" thought provokers to discuss biblical truth with them.

Secondly, use digital devices to supply parents with simple resources they can use to nurture their children spiritually in the daily rhythms of life. For example:

- Send parents a suppertime text message that includes a biblical truth and a simple question about it, such as "Jesus told His disciples to fish on the other side of the boat. That one small change made a huge difference! I wonder what small change Jesus might want each of us to make." The ping their device makes when it receives the text message can remind busy parents to have this spiritually formative conversation!
- Text or email ideas for fun activities parents can enjoy with their kids. Include simple conversation starters. While building a snowman, ask, "Did you know that God is so great that He made every snowflake different from all the rest?" While visiting the zoo, ask, "Did you know that God is so great that He gave every zebra their own pattern of stripes?" While finger-painting, ask, "Did you know that God is so great that He gave each person a different set of fingerprints?"
- Send a short, clear email to parents telling them the Bible story featured in your church's Trail ministry that week. Include the page number in a recommended children's Bible. Supply a couple of simple "I wonder…"

questions. Encourage parents to read and talk about the story with their child one night at bedtime.

Another option is to post blogs and vlogs on parenting. Consider creating your own! Focus on one parenting principle at a time. Illustrate the principle with a real-life story and/or ways to put the principle into practice.

Some general parenting principles include:

- Accept the reality that there is no such thing as a perfect parent.
- Make nurturing your relationship with the Lord, your spouse, and each of your children your top priorities.
- Be the example you want your children to become.
- Love your children with an unconditional love and make sure they feel loved. Every child needs at least one adult who never gives up on them. Spend meaningful time with your child every day and engage them in meaningful conversation. Be interested in what interests them. Express your love with meaningful touch.
- Intentionally use the natural rhythms of life to provide formal and informal spiritual nurture for your children. Point your child beyond their relationship with you to a relationship with God.
- Model prayer at every age.
- Create family traditions that are daily, weekly, seasonal, and even annual. Creating and remembering family traditions writes a family story that gives a child a sense of belonging. In his article "Who We

Are," Jim Burns says that a sense of belonging helps reduce the risk of promiscuous behaviour.[44]

- Adapt your parenting to the different roles you need to play in your child's life as they mature. In the beginning, the child is totally dependent on their parent to supply everything they need. Then the parent needs to be a disciplinarian, exercising authority to keep the child safe and to teach them right from wrong. During the Discover years, the parent becomes more of a nurturer, still teaching but mellowing their authority and leveraging influence by building a good relationship with their child. Wise parents gradually release more responsibility to the child so that during the teen years the parent is more of a coach than a teacher. Finally, when the child becomes a young adult, the parent slides over into the role of an adult friend, no longer leading their child through life but walking beside them to provide plenty of support and wisdom.

And lastly, provide links to help parents access parenting apps and other online resources.

Show parents what your church has to offer and engage them in ongoing conversations. Feature video clips from the Trail ministries on your church website and social media. Give scrolling parents a glimpse of what your church has to offer their family.

Couple promo pieces with opportunities to dialogue. Pose answers to questions parents may be asking, like "What does your church offer for my kids?" and "How well would we fit in?" Continue the dialogue with genuine, caring questions: "What challenges and struggles are you facing as a parent right now? How

---

[44] Jim Burns, "Who We Are," *Children's Ministry Magazine*, January-February 2013.

would you like us to help you? What's the best way for us to communicate with you?"

Provide virtual one-on-one and small group experiences. Zoom and other online meeting apps allow for both one-on-one mentoring and small group discussions which work especially well with Launch kids and parents.

Also consider offering an online mentoring and/or support forum for parenting couples or moms. Dads are usually more inclined to talk with other dads while working on a project or enjoying an activity together.

Grandparents on the Trail

I always felt that my mom was in my corner, except for the one time I thought she had moved to someone else's.

Mom and Dad had come for a visit. We'd finished our evening meal and I volunteered to clean up the kitchen so Mom could play with our preschool daughter. They went off to our daughter's room and spread toys across the bed.

Lost in sudsy water and thoughts a thousand miles away, I put the last dish in the cupboard and checked the time. Discovering that it was long past the children's bedtime, I hustled down the hall to our daughter's room.

"Time to clean up and get ready for bed," I said, sounding like I had my hands on my hips.

As I turned to leave, I heard my mom say in a hushed voice, "That was the warden."

GRANDPARENTS COME IN DIFFERENT SIZES, COLOURS, SHAPES, AND EVEN ages. But there is one thing they all have in common: grandkids and a unique kind of love for them. Children in turn seem to have an innate desire to love and be loved by their grandparents.

Tim and Darcey Kimmel call this love between grandparents and their grandchildren a "grand" love and joke that it may be especially grand because grandparents and their grandchildren share a common enemy: the children's parents![45]

---

[45] Dr. Tim and Darcey Kimmel, *Extreme Grandparenting: The Ride of Your Life* (Carol Stream, IL: Tyndale House, 2007), 16.

Psalm 127:3 tells us that children are a gift from God, and we read in Proverbs 17:6 that grandchildren are a crown.

God has a purpose for the special link between grandparents and their grandkids. He wants to use grandparents to help their grandkids gain His perspective on life.

The Bible says that faith in God is to be passed down from one generation to another. In Psalm 145:4–7, the psalmist says to God, *"One generation commends your works to another."* I like the way The Message translates Psalm 78:4: *"We're not keeping this to ourselves, we're passing it along to the next generation—God's fame and fortune, the marvelous things He has done"* (MSG).

How can grandparents help nurture their grandchildren spiritually? There are at least five practical ways. The more intentional we are with the following five practices, the more spiritually helpful we will be to our grandchildren:

- Spend time with your grandchildren.
- Be an example of someone who is growing in their own relationship with the Lord.
- Talk about God.
- Help the church become a place your children and grandchildren want to be.
- Pray for your children and grandchildren.

Spend time with your grandchildren. It can be hard for grandparents to play a significant role in the lives of their grandchildren when the grandchildren are scattered across the country, or even around the world. Not only are our children and grandchildren mobile, but grandparents today are younger, healthier, more affluent, and therefore mobile too. Grandparents often have plans to travel and pursue their own interests during their retirement years.

Although it may be challenging to play a role in the spiritual nurture of our grandchildren, the need has never been greater. Parents have always been too busy raising their children to enjoy them the same way grandparents can, but the pace parents tend to keep today is even faster and more hectic. Grandparents can be those significant adults who have time for their grandchildren, to listen with their hearts, share hobbies, go on outings, and be present and attentive in a child's life. The stronger our relationship with our grandchildren, the greater our influence will be.

A friend of mine told me this story about her three-year-old granddaughter. It was approaching Christmas and the little girl's mom and dad were financially strapped that year. The dad asked his little girl what she would like most for Christmas and then he held his breath.

The three-year-old thought for a minute. "To go to Grandma's and Grandpa's."

"Okay," the dad said, trying to help them sort out their expectations. "But you know that if you go to Grandma's and Grandpa's, you may not be able to get many toys."

To which his little girl replied, "Daddy, you don't *need* toys at Grandma's and Grandpa's. *They* play with you."

When grandchildren live far away, the grandparents can connect by sending letters and cards in the mail and talking with them on the phone or on the computer. When health permits, grandparents can both visit their grandchildren and invite them to come for visits of their own. One grandchild at a time works well. They'll love having you all to themselves and your home will become a haven of love and safety in a difficult world.

Older grandchildren love receiving care packages. It can be something as simple as hot chocolate and popcorn to enjoy with a movie. Kids of any age like gift certificates for fast food restaurants.

Children need their grandparents in their lives not only for the time and attention grandparents can give, but also for the wisdom God helps grandparents acquire. It's a wisdom born of maturity, experience, and a lifetime of trusting God and learning how to apply His Word.

There's an old saying that says, "If I had known grandchildren would be so much fun, I would have had them first!" But if that were possible, we wouldn't be ready for our grandparenting role. We wouldn't have learned the lessons of faith and obedience we can only learn over time.

Grandchildren and their parents need godly wisdom more than ever. Our grandchildren are growing up in a culture that has turned its back on God. They're being bombarded with trends toward self-indulgence, self-importance, and self-sufficiency. They're being told there is no right and wrong and pushed toward consumerism and immorality.

Our adult children are struggling to know how to raise their children in our secular culture. They need us to come alongside, not to criticize and not to offer unsolicited advice but to offer gentle understanding and loving support.

Be an example of someone who is growing in their own relationship with God. Our grandkids don't need or want us to be perfect. They simply need us to be authentic and open to the transformative work God wants to do within us.

But we do need to keep receiving from the Lord and growing spiritually. We can't give to another something we haven't received ourselves. Sometimes growing spiritually means admitting our mistakes and asking for forgiveness. Asking for forgiveness can have a huge impact on our adult children.

Talk about God. It isn't enough to just live as a Christ follower; we must talk about Him, too. Children are very open and willing to talk about spiritual things. It's usually adults who hide behind all kinds of reasons for keeping quiet.

It really isn't as scary or as difficult as we may think. In the Welcome Circle section of this book, we gave simple examples of a way to begin to talk with children about God. For example, walk around the room with the child and point to everything you see that is red. Say, "I like red. Thank You, God, for giving us pretty colours." Or show the child pictures of animals and say, "God made dogs. God made cats. God made you and me."

It's amazing how the smallest words of witness from those whom children love and respect will stay with them. I once heard of a child who was asked, "How do you know your grandmother loves God?" The child replied, "Because whenever she sends me a birthday card, there's always something from the Bible in it."

Watch and listen for opportunities to explain the choices you make as someone who follows Jesus. Your grandchildren may ask why you've made cookies for your neighbours. Tell them that Jesus wants us to love and help others.

Perhaps an even more effective way to speak intentionally and yet naturally about God is with storytelling. Tell your grandchildren stories of ways God has helped you in the past and how He's helping you in the present. Whenever possible, read Bible stories to your grandchildren and talk with them about what the story teaches us about God. Help them cultivate a thankful heart. Ask them to name things that make them glad. Thank God together for these things.

Our grandchildren need to know that God holds the keys to a rich and meaningful life and that pursuing Him is the way to experience it.

Help the church become a place your children and grandchildren want to be. The world has changed so rapidly in our lifetime that it's affected what younger people look for in a church. This hurts us because we tend to love the familiar.

It's natural for us to be afraid of change. We may even feel angry that the way we've always done things is being challenged. We may feel sad over what's being lost and need to grieve.

But at some point, if we care about the spiritual nurture of our children and grandchildren, we will have to ask how we can be the kind of church they'll want to attend. Visionary leaders challenge grandparents with this thought: "If your children and grandchildren lived far away, wouldn't you want a church near them, without compromising the Gospel, to become the kind of church they would want to attend?"

Pray for your children and grandchildren. The most important thing anyone can do for their children and grandchildren is to pray for them, regularly and fervently. Ask God to give them a close relationship with Him. Imagine what their life would be like if they lived with God at the centre of it and ask God to accomplish those things in their lives. Pray that they will know and love Jesus. Pray for their parents, friends, teachers, and caregivers and for their health and safety. Pray for God's purposes to be fulfilled in your grandchildren's lives. Ask for their prayer requests. Pray with them, in person or on the phone.

Pray for God to be at work in your adult child's life and in your relationship with them. If you find yourself wishing you had done a better job nurturing your own children spiritually, realize that God has given you a second chance with your grandchildren. God can work through you and your grandchildren to help your adult children.

Immersing the Trail in Intergenerational Ministry

One Friday night at family camp, we projected a full-length children's movie on the outside wall of the lodge. It was chilly under the black, star-studded sky, so we wrapped ourselves in blankets before snuggling into our lawn chairs. Someone had made salty, buttery popcorn and passed it around in big buckets.

There were kids of all ages, moms and dads, grandmas and grandpas; we were like one huge family. The sense of belonging was palatable.

I'm sure the cozy togetherness resonated with the children, but for them there was an added thrill: sharing the fun with adults.

My favourite memories of being on our trails here in Atlantic Canada include hiking, biking, and snowshoe adventures. Each experience has been about much more than the trail itself. It's been about being immersed in fresh, invigorating air. It's been about being caught up in delightful smells and sounds. It's been about breathtaking scenery—roaring oceans crashing against rocky cliffs, soft rolling farmland, and snow-covered trees.

Following the trails has been about taking steps on the ground beneath my feet, but it's also been about something much less precise: the intangible effect the environment around the Trail has had on me.

The influence of what surrounds the Trail is much broader than the Trail itself and it affects me in deeper ways. It enhances the whole experience, turning physical exercise into something that influences and forms my soul. Just as our experiences on physical trails are enhanced by the natural environment, our experiences on the spiritual formation Trail will be enhanced when they're surrounded by a vibrant intergenerational faith community.

What is an intergenerational faith community? An intergenerational faith community is a gathered people of multiple generations—there can be as many as five from birth to old age—who pursue God individually and corporately.

The gathering is intergenerational when different generations are engaged in the same activity. It's a faith community when shared faith in God motivates and infiltrates the gathering. It's a community when members of each represented generation interact with, respect, enjoy, care about, work with, and learn from and with members of other generations.

Intergenerational faith communities are essential to spiritual formation. It has always been God's plan that faith in Him be passed down from one generation to another (Psalm 45:17, Psalm 71:18, Psalm 78:4–6, Psalm 89:1, Psalm 145:4). It was the way God's chosen people lived. Hebrew grandparents, aunts and uncles, parents, young adults, and children came together to recite the Torah and share traditional stories of God and their faith in Him.

When New Testament followers of Jesus assembled, they were the very old, the very young, and everyone in between. Children learned by being with people of every age to experience life, talk about life, and learn about trusting God with life—together.

I love to imagine the spiritual lessons children would have learned the night Paul said goodbye to the Ephesians elders on the beach at Miletus (Acts 20:13–38). Perhaps the women and children stayed home with extended family while the elders (men) made the trip from Ephesus to Miletus.

But I like to think that the women and children wanted to be with Paul, too. Paul knew he would never see these beloved believers again. He was on his way to Jerusalem, the Holy Spirit having forewarned him that prisons and hardships lay ahead. As

Paul said goodbye to this little band of elders, he urged them to become leaders and shepherds over the flock he was leaving behind.

Imagine how the final scenes of this drama would have affected any children who were there:

> *When Paul had finished speaking, he knelt down with all of them and prayed. They all wept as they embraced him and kissed him. What grieved them most was his statement that they would never see his face again. Then they accompanied him to the ship.*
>
> —Acts 20:36–38

If you had been one of the children present, would you have hung back, pressed into silence by the adults' sadness? Or would you have been tugging on an adult's hand, your father's or your grandfather's perhaps, wanting to know, "Where is Paul going? Why can't he stay here with us? Why does God want him to go? Why are you so sad? What do we do now?"

If that reflective exercise stirred your spirit, imagine what it would have been like for children who were present when young Eutychus fell out of the upstairs window! Even if children in that crowded upstairs room had fallen asleep, I'm sure the commotion would have woken them! (Acts 20:7–12)

As John Roberto writes in "Our Future Is Intergenerational," we are beginning to return to intergenerational practises and expressions of the church. Just as God has been calling us back to the importance of the parenting role in spiritual formation, so He is calling us to become more intentional about intergenerational ministry. As Roberto puts it, "something old is new again."[46]

I would never want to disrespect the mystery of God's supernatural ways by trying to oversimplify them, but to help us

---

46 John Roberto, "Our Future Is Intergenerational," *Christian Education Journal*, series 3, volume 9, no.1, 2012, 105.

understand why intergenerational dynamics may be so powerful in spiritual formation, consider again Larry Richards's principles for effective role-modelling.[47] If we look at the faith community not only as reinforcements for the role-modelling parents do, but also as multiple role-modelling relationships for every child, we can begin to grasp the power of it.

It isn't enough to simply bring the generations together in one room. The principles for effective role-modelling must be intentionally applied. For example, it's critical that the relationships between members of different generations be warm and loving.

I have always felt that the West End Baptist Church—now known as The Crossing Church, where our kids did most of their growing up—helped us raise them. For the thirteen years we lived in Newfoundland, the people at West End were an extended family for us. We enjoyed plenty of fun intergenerational events together with adults and children, teens and young adults all playing and serving and learning as one.

Adults of every age also consistently engaged kids in conversation after worship on Sunday mornings. The adults were genuinely interested and lovingly supportive of the younger people in the church. They asked about their interests, prayed for them, and stepped aside to let young people use their developing gifts to lead, serve, and teach others.

And this wasn't just at church. Our Newfoundland church members often hosted gatherings in their homes. Children, teenagers, and young adults were always included in the fun and conversation. I know Newfoundlanders are famous for their commitment to family and hospitality, but the way they do church doesn't have to be unique. It can serve as a model for other faith communities.

We will have to be intentional about pursuing this model. Even though there seems to be a new desire for intergenerational

---

47 See Appendix 4: Larry Richard's Seven Principles for Effective Role-Modelling.

faith experiences, they tend to be countercultural in our society. Our educational and recreational systems are almost exclusively divided into age groups. Generations within families, and consequently in society, tend to be separated by individualism, greater mobility, and financial independence.

Intergenerational faith experiences are not only countercultural, they can also be challenging, noisy, and messy. We may need to add intergenerational experiences gradually, the way we build other aspects of the Trail, helping adults learn to flow with the noisy, messy parts while helping them discover the gift of joy in young faces, thoughts, hearts, and energy over time.

Consider starting with a bubble of a couple of families and seniors who gather in a home to pray and reflect on Scripture in child-friendly ways.

Try an intergenerational worship service. Involve children and youth as leaders. Help parents relax with spoken and written assurances that their children are welcome, wiggles and all. Provide tactile listening aids for the children and encourage speakers to use smaller words.

Host church family meals with planned seating that brings different generations together around the tables. Provide questions to stimulate conversation and perhaps also tabletop games or crafts.

Provide intergenerational seasonal events. Bring people of every age together at informal Christmas concerts, sunrise Easter services, and Thanksgiving pumpkin events.

Run family camps, whether they're overnight or even just day-long events, where multiple generations can experience life together and make special memories. Include horseback riding or homemade versions of popular game shows like *Family Feud*.

Engage people of every age in missional service projects. Doing missional service individually is a valuable witness, but when we strike out on our own, our neighbours might simply chalk it up to us being nice people.

Imagine a team of people, of every age, working together to help make positive changes in other peoples' lives. Wouldn't our neighbours sit up and take notice? Wouldn't they be wondering, "Who are these people?" Wouldn't that be a wonderful way to introduce them to Jesus?

The age-appropriate spiritual formation sections, intentional spiritual nurture at home, and intergenerational surroundings of the Trail aren't mutually exclusive. Think all/and. Let the principles of each flow from one to the other. Effective spiritual formation of children, and all of us, is supernaturally mysterious and more complex than a single approach.

Ceremony of Promise and Blessing
Appendix 1

Many parents, including those with little or no church experience, come asking for opportunities to dedicate their children to God. Sometimes these parents don't know what they're asking. Perhaps they're familiar with infant baptism, whether their own or someone else's. Often there is a sense that bringing their baby to the church for some sort of initiation rite will secure their baby's salvation. What a wonderful opportunity to teach young parents more about God, salvation by faith in Jesus, and parenting!

Your church can offer a Ceremony of Promise and Blessing for parents and their babies. A Ceremony of Promise and Blessing is an event conducted by the church to give parents the opportunity to promise before God and other witnesses that they will, with God's help and to the best of their ability, raise their newborn child to know God.

But the parents aren't the only ones who make promises. The church promises to support the parents and partner with them in the spiritual nurture of their child. The ceremony is also an opportunity to pray God's blessing on the baby, asking God to favour the child. Assure parents that making these promises doesn't mean forcing their children to become Christians. Rather it means creating an environment that will help their children make good choices about their relationship with God.

Older siblings can be included in the ceremony—or, if they have already been blessed in a service of their own, older children can stand with their parents as part of the family and be affirmed in their role as a big brother or sister. Sometimes parents invite extended family members or close friends to stand with them on the platform during the ceremony to indicate their personal support. Sometimes one of these close relatives or friends leads in prayer or sings a meaningful song.

At the end of the ceremony, it is appropriate to gift parents with a parenting resource. *The Beginner's Bible* is a popular choice.[48]

When parents who aren't yet Christians hear an explanation of a Ceremony of Promise and Blessing, they often realize that they themselves are not spiritually ready to make the parenting commitments they will be asked to make during the ceremony. Pray that this realization will spur them on toward Christ. Encourage them to start their spiritual journey by becoming engaged in your faith community.

Even though children grow fast, try not to rush parents into a Ceremony of Promise and Blessing. Sometimes parents need time to take stock of their own spiritual needs. Sometimes parents are still so tired and overwhelmed by the birth of their baby that they can't absorb teaching about parenting. We don't want preparation for the ceremony or the ceremony itself to become one more blur in their sleep-deprived days!

When parents are ready for a Ceremony of Promise and Blessing, help them prepare for it by meeting with them to discuss the promises they'll be making. A simple outline of some parenting principles for spiritual formation can help guide the discussion.[49]

Here is a sample Ceremony of Promise and Blessing. After the ceremony, gift the parents with a resource like *The Beginner's Bible*, a copy of the Ceremony of Promise and Blessing, and a copy of the "Godly Parenting" brochure.[50]

---

[48] Karyn Henley, *The Beginner's Bible* (Grand Rapids, MI: Zondervan, 2016).
[49] See Appendix 2: Principles for Godly Parenting.
[50] Ibid.

Ceremony of Promise and Blessing
at
(Name of Church)
on
(Date of Ceremony)
for
(Child's Name)
Born: *(Date of Birth)*

It's time now for our Ceremony of Promise and Blessing. I invite *(parents' names and child's name)* to join me here on the platform.

This is a precious time of promising to do all we can to raise a child to know and love Jesus. It is also a sacred time of asking God to bless the child.

Introduction. *(Parents' names)* have come today to promise God, in our presence, to provide spiritual nurture for their child. And they have brought their daughter/son, *(child's name)*, for a prayer of blessing. Welcome, *(parents' names and child's name)*.

(Parents' names), you are doing a wonderful thing. By standing here, you are declaring, like Joshua, *"But as for me and my household, we will serve the Lord"* (Joshua 24:15).

We realize that promising to do all you can to help your child know and love Jesus is huge, but we also know that you won't have to do it alone. As you lean into God, He will be your strength and wisdom, help you be the authentic Christ-followers that *(child's name)* needs to see, and be at work in *(child's name)*'s life.

The promise to provide spiritual nurture for your child can seem overwhelming when you think of all the parenting years to come, but God wants you to take it just one day, even just one opportunity, at a time.

In Deuteronomy 6:5–7, God gives us a beautiful plan for providing spiritual nurture in the natural rhythms of everyday life:

Love the Lord your God with all your heart and with all your soul and with all your strength. These commandments that I give you today are to be on your hearts. Impress them on your children. Talk about them when you sit at home and when you walk along the road, when you lie down and when you get up.

Thank you for the visit we had as we prepared for this Ceremony. During that visit, we talked about intentional, child-friendly ways in which you can help *(child's name)* experience God in regular parts of his/her day. God bless you as weave these practices into your lives.

The parents' promise. And now let me ask you some questions so you can seal your promise with your responses.

Pastor: *(Parents' names)*, do you promise to do all you can to help *(child's name)* know and love Jesus?
Parents: We do.
Pastor: Do you promise to turn to God for His help with both your own spiritual journey and parenting?
Parents: We do.
Pastor: Do you promise to make the Bible, prayer, having conversations about God, and connecting with other believers part of the regular rhythm of your lives?
Parents: We do.

The church's promise. God never intended for parents to raise their children on their own. He draws us into intergenerational faith communities so we can help one another on our spiritual journeys and help parents pass faith on to their children.

It might be tempting for parents to think they don't need the church, or for both parents and the church to think it is up to the church alone to provide all the spiritual nurture a child needs, but neither of these extremes is healthy. God wants parents and the church to form a dynamic partnership.

Pastor: *(Name of church)*, will you promise to do all you can to help these parents with *(child's name)*'s spiritual nurture? If so, please stand.

Church: Father God, please help us to keep the promises we are making here today. Help us to partner with *(parents' names)* to help *(child's name)* know You and love You. Help us to honour You by doing the same with all the parents and children in our care. Amen.

Pastor: You may be seated.

The blessing. We are told that Jesus *"took the children in his arms, placed his hands on them and blessed them"* (Mark 10:16). The word "blessing" signifies asking God's favour upon a person.

Father God, thank You for *(child's name)*, for she/he is marvellously made and a wondrous creation of body and soul. Thank You for blessing *(parents' names)* with her/him.

And now, may God our Father bless you, *(child's name)*. May the grace of Christ and the power of the Holy Spirit rest upon you all the days of your life. Amen.

Principles for Godly Parenting
Appendix 2

But grow in the grace and knowledge of our Lord and Savior Jesus Christ. To him be glory both now and forever! Amen.
—2 Peter 3:18

Be the example you want your child to imitate. Love God with all your heart, soul, and mind and honour Him with the choices you make.

Do your kids see you setting aside time to spend alone with the Lord? Do they see you leaning into God for help with the challenges you face in your day-to-day life? Do they see you honouring God with your finances? Do they see you honouring God with your entertainment and media choices? Do they see you managing your time to protect the priorities God wants you to have?

You will always be the greatest influence in your children's lives, even when they're teens and listening to other voices. Children learn things most readily from their parents' example. This is how God designed parenting to work. We will never be a perfect example, but when we make mistakes we can model humility by asking for forgiveness (sometimes from our children) and God's help to do better.

Love your spouse. Give your kids a good example of a healthy marriage. Work on your marriage. Show love and respect for each other, work together as partners, be one another's best friend, "fight right," have fun together, and ask for help when you need it.

A strong marriage gives your kids emotional security. It is helpful for them to know that after God, you are first in each other's lives. Remember that you aren't only giving your children roots, but also wings. One day your children will leave the nest and you and your spouse will want to be one another's best friend. Also, healthy marriages breed healthy marriages… by example.

Love your child. Nurture your relationship with your child. Spend time with them to enjoy them and to allow them to enjoy you. Listen with your full attention. Be there as much as you can for those times when they're ready to talk. Share experiences together and let them see you making God-honouring choices. Explain to them why you make the choices you do. Demonstrate practical faith.

Build trust and respect into your relationship with each of your children and receive from them a willingness to listen to you and learn from you. Enjoy regular memory-making times as a family but also be intentional about spending one-on-one time with each child.

As our children grow, so does the nature of our parenting relationship with them. We move from nurturer and disciplinarian to coach in their teen years, and then to adult friend in their young adulthood.

Not only do we need to parent according to our children's different ages, we also need to keep their unique personalities in mind and parent accordingly. When parents manage their relationships well with their children, their children tend to turn to them for advice throughout their adult lives.

Train your child with "course corrections." In her book *Spiritual Parenting*, Michelle Anthony outlines four important steps for making "course corrections." Course corrections is Michelle's phrase for helping your child learn from the experience when they do something wrong.

1. Allow your child to feel the pain of wrongdoing. Be consistent with consequences such as loss of privileges.
2. Assure your child of your unconditional love and affection for them.
3. Talk with your child about the better choices they could have made.
4. Affirm your child. Assure them you are confident that they will make a better choice next time.[51]

Pray for your child. Ask God for help with day-to-day situations as they arise. Pray into your children's future, asking God to lead them to faith in Jesus, the right mate, and God's calling and purpose for their lives.

Partner with your church. Show your children that engagement in the faith community is a protected priority for you and help them think through their choices to make it so for them.

As they grow older, they need other voices saying the same things you are saying to them. And they need the steadying, encouraging example of peers who share their faith in God.

Engaging in the faith community will also help them discover their God-given gifts and God's purpose for their lives. Teach your children not to allow the pressures of our affluent, success-driven society to crowd out their commitment to and engagement in the faith community.

Nurture your child spiritually in the regular rhythms of day-to-day life. We read in Deuteronomy 6:5–7 a guide for how to model spirituality in your children's everyday lives. The phrase *"when you sit at home"* indicates opportunities you may have while eating meals or doing chores together to have natural conversations with your child about God.

---

51 Michelle Anthony, *Spiritual Parenting* (Colorado Springs, CO: David C. Cook, 2010), 158–164.

Use "I wonder..." statements. For example, "I wonder what God would say about..." Also, ask questions such as "How has God helped you today? Is there anyone or anything you would like us to pray for?" Then share your own faith experiences: "I read this in the Bible today. I like what God says about..." Memorize Scripture together as a family. When you watch a movie together, talk about it from God's perspective.

The phrase *"when you lie down"* refers to bedtime. Teach your children the habit of bedtime devotions when they're young by reading a Bible story and praying together. Help them transition into their own time alone with God when they are preteens.

The phrase *"when you walk along the road"* can refer to walks or time spent together in the car. Use this time to enjoy good Christian music, pray for people and places as you pass, and enjoy good discussions. Don't fill the air with your words; listen carefully as your children share their thoughts.

The phrase *"when you get up"* refers to waking up in the morning. Bless your child with a word of encouragement or prayer. Ask, "How can I pray for you today?"

There is no such thing as a perfect parent. There will be bad days, nasty episodes, and challenging seasons. As long as the overall note is right and parents keep their eyes on God and are intentional about godly parenting, God can be trusted with the rest.

What our children need most are authentic parents who keep growing spiritually. Realizing how ill equipped we are to raise our children keeps us dependent on God. Depending on God takes us back to the first principle of godly parenting and helps us become the spiritually growing example our children need to see.

It's never too late for our children to make course corrections. It's never too late for us to do the same.

Sample Child Protection Policy
Appendix 3

Our child protection policy is intended to make our church a safer place for children and youth. In addition to their safety, which is our first concern, this plan is intended to enhance the spiritual growth and development of children and youth—since we all learn better when our primary needs are being met—reassure parents and grandparents, and provide protective boundaries for individuals on our ministry teams.

Our protection plan has five main components:

- Screening
- Supervision
- Reporting allegations
- Training for Ministry Teams
- Further Health and Safety Restrictions and Guidelines

Screening

All persons working with children/youth must:
1. Be in Grade Nine or older.
2. Attend our church for at least six months before joining a ministry team that works with children and/or youth. University students and students from other postsecondary institutions may practice sooner but only with supervision for the first six months.

3. Be interviewed by one of our pastoral staff or ministry team leaders.
4. Complete a ministry team application form.
5. Submit a current (every five years) police background check. A record involving any abuse of children, or of any persons or animals, will in all cases disqualify the individual from working with children or youth through this church.
6. Participate in a protection plan orientation session.

Supervision

All persons working with children/youth must:
1. Never be alone with a child/youth. Even if there is only one child/youth present, there must be at least two ministry team members present. Because these two ministry team members must be objective witnesses for one another, they cannot be from the same family.
2. Make all ministry activity visible. Avoid isolated spaces. Keep opaque doors open and bar the threshold to the room with baby gates or half-doors. Keep windows in doors uncovered so everything that is happening in the room can be easily seen from the corridor. Move to a quiet spot within the room for a private conversation with a minor, but do not leave the room. Ministry team members must call parents for diaper changes unless we have written permission from the parent to do diaper changes.
3. Only touch a child appropriately, specifically on the hand, arm, or shoulder. Direct children who want to sit on your lap to sit beside you. Give sideways

hugs, A-frame hugs (only cheeks touch), or quick release hugs.

4. Insist that children ask permission before leaving the group to use the washroom. All children up to Grade Six who leave to use the washroom must be accompanied by a ministry team member. The ministry team member must first ensure that there is no one else in the washroom and then send the child in alone. The ministry team member must stand with their back against the door opened to the corridor and guide the child with their voice. If the child needs help, the ministry team member must ask someone else to enter the washroom with them and/or send someone for the child's parents. Ministry team members must have a parent's written consent before they can take a child who is being toilet-trained to the washroom.

5. Ensure that all children up to and including Grade Twelve are registered. Registration forms must be signed by the child/youth's parent/guardian.

6. Ensure that all children up to and including Grade Five are signed into our Sunday morning and weekday children's ministries by the adult who brings them. The adult who brings the child must indicate in writing the name of the person who will pick up the child.

7. Be responsible for the safety of every child until the adult responsible for the child arrives at the ministry space to pick them up. Parents, grandparents, or the adult who brings the child must arrive immediately after worship or other adult event to reassume responsibility for their child. They must sign to show

that they are the person who is supposed to be picking up the child.
8. Ensure that children/youth being transported to church ministry events in either a private vehicle, taxi, or bus are accompanied by at least two responsible adults. A child/youth may travel in a car with only one adult only if the child's parent or guardian has given written permission and only if there are other children or youth in the car as well.
9. Ensure that pictures and names of children are not published without parental permission.
10. Ensure that the location of overnight events are not made public.
11. Keep a record of all online communication with youth.

Reporting Allegations

1. Any adult who has reasonable grounds to believe that a child or youth has been subjected to abusive behaviour will:
    - listen carefully to what a child/youth says without asking questions or making notes. You may make notes immediately afterwards, but not in the minor's presence.
    - never promise not to tell anyone. Assure the child that you will only tell someone if the child or someone else needs help.
    - report what the child/youth says and/or any other concerns or observations of possible abuse to one of the pastors, who must then see that the

Department of Social Development is contacted. If the accusation is against one of the pastors, the lead pastor must also contact our denominational office. If the accusation is about the lead pastor, the report must first be made to the chair of the council, who will then see that the Department of Social Development and our denominational office are contacted.

2. A written copy of every report, including dates, times, and content of all pertinent conversations, will be kept in a confidential file in a pastor's office. These reports must be kept indefinitely regardless of the outcome of any subsequent investigation.
3. If it is proven that child abuse by a member of the church has taken place, he/she will be required to step down from all leadership positions. However, the church will practice discipline according to Matthew 18:15–17, maintaining frequent communication and supportive relationships with those suspected or guilty of child abuse as long as these persons demonstrate willingness to listen, change, and look to Christ for help.
4. The church will ask the Department of Social Development if it can assist in helping both hurting families. This doesn't include the need for hurting individuals to receive professional counselling.
5. Our church is only responsible to make a report if the person allegedly abused is eighteen years or younger. Our church takes all allegations seriously but is not responsible to make a report if the person allegedly abused is now an adult.

Training Ministry Teams

1. All new ministry team members must complete a child protection orientation session with a pastor or ministry team leader before they join a ministry team that works with minors. The content of this orientation session will include reasons why a child protection plan is important, a review of our written protection policy, and discussion about the importance and implication of each aspect of the policy.
2. This child protection plan will be reviewed and updated at least once a year. Copies of the document posted on the website will be refreshed.
3. Ministry team training will review and evaluate the specific ways in which our church's child protection plan is being implemented in their particular ministry, and commit to any changes that must be made for greater effectiveness.
4. A printed copy of an updated child protection policy document will be made available to ministry team members who work with minors, as well as to parents, grandparents, and other adults who bring children to the church.

Further Health and Safety Restrictions and Guidelines

1. If a child is not well enough to participate in the group or displays symptoms of contagious illness, the parent/guardian will be asked to take them home.
2. Ministry team leaders will not give children medications. Exceptions will be reviewed on a case-by-case basis.

3. Ministry teams will be advised, at least annually, as to the location of first aid kits.
4. In the case of an incident, ministry team members who witness the incident must complete a written incident report and file the report with a pastor. Incident report forms are kept in the photocopier room. Incidents include any kind of accident of physical mishap such as a fall; a scrape; a cut; a bruise; two children hitting, kicking, or otherwise hurting or fighting with each other; or a child running away from a ministry team member or going missing even temporarily, etc.
5. Fire evacuation and lockdown plans will be reviewed at least annually in ministry team training. Specific evacuation directions will be posted in each room.

I have read this policy and agree with it.

_____

Signature   Date

Larry Richards's Seven Principles for Effective Role-Modelling

Appendix 4

One of the things I have learned over the years is that God is big on principles. He hasn't anchored practices the way He has principles. Practices, the way we apply principles, can and should change to keep the church relevant in our ever-changing world, but principles are timeless. They are timeless because they are profound and true. Everything we do should be based on trustworthy principles.

The fact that God has designed spiritual formation to be intergenerational is a trustworthy principle. So is God's intention that parents be His most effective agents in the spiritual formation of their children.

These two principles are supported by the truths Larry Richards discovered in his research about effective role-modelling. A few years ago, I rediscovered these seven principles for effective role-modelling in one of Larry Richards' books, a text we used when I was in seminary.

1. There needs to be frequent, long-term contact with the model(s).
2. There needs to be a warm, loving relationship with the model(s).
3. There needs to be exposure to the inner state of the model(s). [Models need to talk about the thoughts and feelings that affect their behaviour.]
4. The model(s) needs to be observed in a variety of life settings and situations.

5. The model(s) needs to exhibit consistency and clarity in behavior, values, etc.
6. There needs to be a correspondence between the behavior of the model(s) and the beliefs [ideal standards] of the community. [That is, the faith community, the church.]
7. There needs to be explanation of the lifestyle of the model(s) conceptually with instruction accompanying shared experiences. [We experience something together and I tell you about the convictions that led to the choice I made. For example, the cashier at the grocery store slips something in my bag without zapping the barcode. I take it out of my bag and give it to him to ring through. I explain that taking it without paying for it would be dishonest and God wants us to be honest.][52]

Reflection and Discussion

1. How do these principles support the idea that parents are the most effective agents for spiritual formation?
2. How have these principles been verified by the way God has used role models in your life?
3. How can children's ministry pastors and volunteers apply these principles in their relationships with children and youth?
4. How can these principles be woven into the practices of your church?

---

52 Lawrence O. Richards, *A Theology of Children's Ministry* (Grand Rapids, MI: Zondervan, 1983), 78.

Helping Parents with Discipline
Appendix 5

Typically we think of discipline as punishment. It is much more helpful to think of discipline as training, the kind of training in righteous or right thinking and behaviour that God gives us as our heavenly Father.

God disciplines us because He loves us and wants something better for us. Loving our child will mean selflessly following through with discipline even though we are tired, busy, or consumed with our own issues.

Parents need to be intentional about consistently giving their child the right kind of training, because this helps develop their character and prepare them for life. Parents who mistakenly think their primary task is to make their child happy may not understand the importance of discipline. But avoiding loving correction isn't the way to raise happy children. Such an approach can lead a parent to raise demanding, ungrateful, and entitled individuals who never assume responsibility for themselves.

It also helps to think of the way our heavenly Father provides this discipline for us so we can follow His example. God always disciplines us in a loving way, showing us the wrong we have done and helping us understand how to make a better choice next time. He doesn't yell and scream when we make a wrong choice. He is gentle but firm. His discipline is never about venting His own anger, but about shaping us.

He doesn't always rescue us from the painful consequences of wrong we have done because the pain helps to teach us. However,

He is quick to forgive us when we name the wrong and always there to help us next time.

The disciplining we do as parents needs to be bathed in prayer. We can't discipline effectively without God's help, and our children can't make the right choices without God's help. Disciplining our children is a great opportunity to teach them how utterly dependent we all need to be on God.

Michelle Anthony, author of *Spiritual Parenting*, builds her approach to godly discipline on a foundation of spiritual formation and calls the approach "course corrections."[53] A couple of Anthony's ideas, and certainly the spirit of them, show up in the following list of messages conveyed by godly discipline:

- You are safe with me. I have established boundaries that keep you safe and I will help you stay within them.
- I love you no matter what. After we talk about the wrong you did, I will open my arms and you can crawl onto my lap and be close to my heart because my heart is always overflowing with love for you.
- You can do this! You are called to live God's way, and you can make the choices He wants you to make with His help. What will you ask God to help you do next time you face this choice?
- You are acquiring self-discipline through the training I provide.
- You are responsible for your own life and your own choices. I am not. Therefore, I will not always rescue you from the consequences of your choices.

---

53 Anthony, *Spiritual Parenting*, 158–164.

Practical Suggestions for Disciplining Your Child

None of the following suggestions are wholly original. I have gathered them from many sources over the years. Some even date back to Dr. Clyde M. Narramore, a Christian psychologist who wrote for parents many years ago. I have tried and tested these suggestions and found them to be excellent advice.

1. Be sure your child is getting enough positive attention. Our children have a primary need to know that we want them, love them, and see them.
2. Be careful not to confuse mistakes and natural childishness with willful disobedience. Be patient with natural childishness and learn to enjoy it. It won't last!
3. If you take something away from your toddler that they were playing with, give them something else to play with.
4. Let children choose between two good things. For example, "Would you like an apple or an orange?"
5. Remember that your child is apt to misbehave if they're bored. Engage them in a new activity. Sometimes children are ready for new challenges before we realize it!
6. Let children rest when they're tired.
7. Ignore tantrums. They don't last long without an audience. Sometimes it's best to simply leave the room.
8. Give your child positive direction rather than negative commands. The word "don't" brings out the rebel in all of us!
9. Nurture good behaviour with helpful routines. For example, "Get into your pyjamas and brush your teeth. Then you can have a bedtime story."

10. Expect children to obey.
11. Slow down and maintain eye contact with your child.
12. Ask questions to be sure your child understands what you are asking them to do.
13. Be careful not to over-rely on timeouts. They can be used effectively to help a child recover from pouting, crying, or a temper tantrum, but there are often more natural or logical consequences for acts of disobedience. Plus, too many timeouts can cause feelings of isolation or rejection. Rather than sending a child to a timeout, it may be more helpful to join them in listening to quiet music or in a calming activity like colouring.
14. Establish clear boundaries, far enough away to give your child space but close enough to provide safety. For example, "You can play in our yard or in your friend's yard next door, but you must not cross the street or play in any other yard." The older our children get, the more we need to negotiate boundaries and consequences with them.
15. Work with your child's temperament. For example, if your child is strong-willed, say "You're in charge of cleaning up!" If your child has a playful temperament, say, "Let's make cleaning up a game!" Give your calm, loving child plenty of notice by saying, "You have five more minutes and then we'll have to clean up." Encourage your perfectionist by saying, "You're doing a great job with clean-up!"[54]
16. Ask children to apologize and let them know you expect it, but don't force it. Our kids will best learn

---

54 Capehart, West, and West, *The Discipline Guide for Children's Ministry*, 55, 57, 60, 62.

apologizing from us. When we wrong them, we need to admit the mistake directly to them, tell them we're sorry, and ask them to forgive us. And we need to model this in all our other relationships.
17. Keep acts of discipline between you and your child as much as possible. Correcting them in front of their friends or others causes shame.
18. Work with your kids to resolve predictable challenges, such as sharing the use of the computer, television, etc.
19. Aim to be consistently firm and consistently loving. Parents tend to switch back and forth between two extremes: being as rigid as a wall or as soft as a jellyfish. It helps to know that our children both need and expect a firm "No" when something is dangerous, unloving/immoral, or unhealthy. Our carefully considered nos help them feel safe. If we don't say no when they intuitively know we should, they will feel vulnerable and confused. But we should only say no when a no is necessary. Say yes whenever you can!

Helping Parents Nurture Good Relationships with Their Children

Appendix 6

Kids will always respond best to spiritual nurture and discipline when these are given in the context of a loving relationship.

This is especially true for Discover children for whom relationships are developmentally and fundamentally key. Children this age will remember the overall feeling of the experience and the relationship more than what is said.

But just when children most need flourishing relationships with their parents, when they start school and especially during their Launch or preteen years, parents tend to get busy with other things.

Well-meaning parents also tend to push their children into too much busyness. Parents struggle with their own particular kind of peer pressure when, worried that their child will somehow be left behind, they enroll their child in every extracurricular activity other parents choose for their children. It's not that children shouldn't be engaged in extracurricular activities; it's that hectic schedules, ours and our children's, can rob us of the kind of quantitative and qualitative time needed to nurture close relationships at home.

Balance is key. Keep your family healthy and wholesome by regularly evaluating and adjusting family commitments. As you work toward balance, consider the seasons of life. Some days seem long when we're caring for young children, but the years when they're young go by fast!

Build trust by spending time together. Here are some simple ways to nurture your relationship with your young school-age children as you intentionally spend time with them.

Have fun doing things with your child that they like to do. For example, colour together. Play house together. Build with Lego together.

Read aloud with your child and make this a special time. For example, save chapter books for Saturday nights.

Do bedtime devotions with your child and then linger. There may be an intimate conversation waiting to happen. From time to time, ask, "What did you see God doing today? Was there something you did today that you wish you could do differently?"

Do chores together. For example, follow a recipe to cook or bake something, or do laundry. You may find it helpful to follow these classic steps for teaching an apprentice:

- I do, you watch. We talk.
- I do, you help. We talk.
- You do, I help. We talk.
- You do, I watch. We talk.

Be active together. For example, ride bikes or go tobogganing.

Serve someone else together. For example, visit a senior, provide childcare for a new mom, or bake cookies for a neighbour.

Find fun ways to memorize Scripture together at the supper table.

Take your child with you when you run errands. Include a treat! Help them learn people skills by watching you. Explain your choices to teach a biblical worldview.

Collect things together. Kids this age love collecting things. Consider collecting things that won't fit into a box. When our children were young, we spent our summer vacations at a family cottage on Prince Edward Island and collected lighthouses. We'd jump in the car with a picnic lunch, follow the map to a lighthouse we had never seen before, explore the lighthouse, take a picture of it, and then go home and paste the picture in a scrapbook. It was hours of fun for everyone! We had friends who collected covered bridges.

Sort things together, such as canned goods, linens, and clothing. Kids this age love sorting things, which is good news for cupboards and closets that need an overhaul!

Do something in the same room while they do their homework. For example, do the dishes, delete old emails, etc.

Include your children in social events with adult friends and relatives. Do things together with other families.

Set up a jigsaw puzzle, one that's not too hard, and invite your child to work on it with you, perhaps for a short while before bedtime each evening. Look for jigsaw puzzles that have large, medium, and small pieces.

Save one night a week for fun family times. Play games, go on outings, and use your imagination to come up with fun ideas. If you watch a movie together, talk about the values that are depicted in the movie. Make a rule that no one, including parents, can take phone calls, texts, or otherwise use their electronic devices during family night. Be with the people you are with!

Talk with your child. Authors Reggie Joiner and Carey Nieuwhof encourage parents to "learn to communicate in a style that values the relationship" they have with their child.[55]

Our words carry a lot of influence. We need God's help to make them life-giving. When you talk with your child:

- Even though it seems counterintuitive, listen more than you talk.
- Put yourself in your child's shoes and try to remember how you felt when you were their age.

---

55 Joiner and Nieuwhof, *Parenting Beyond Your Capacity*, 107.

- Remember not to force the conversation. If you are nearby and available, your child can initiate conversation when they feel ready to talk.
- Remember that some children, boys especially, will be more apt to talk while you work on something together.
- Follow up on things your child told you earlier.
- Try making comments instead of asking questions.
- Accept your child's theology. It can be sorted out later. For example, don't correct your child if she says, "I let Jesus have a turn on my swing today."
- Acknowledge and validate your child's feelings. If they have a problem, help them think through ways of handling it.
- Be willing to talk about whatever is on your child's mind, even if you don't know the answers.
- Make faith real by sharing how you trust God with the hard stuff.

Help your children to process scary news. Most parents want to protect their children from the issues of our fallen world. But it's becoming increasingly difficult in our media-saturated culture to preserve childlike innocence.

Children overhear news about bombings, shootings, wars, and natural disasters. Sometimes tragedy strikes a child's own family or a family in the neighbourhood where they live. The COVID-19 pandemic made unsettling newsfeeds a regular part of all our lives.

It's tempting for us parents to want to believe our children are oblivious to the trauma, but the truth is that children are very much aware. In *People in Process*, author Maxine Hancock wrote that we should multiply what we think our children know about what's going on by ten—and she wrote that a very long time ago![56]

When something unsettling happens, we must not ignore our children. It's important for them to be able to verbalize their fears and concerns and for us to take what they're feeling seriously. If we don't help children deal with reality, their imaginations will undoubtedly make it even worse than it is.

What is the best way for parents to approach these talks? Sally Lloyd-Jones shares the following principles:

- Let children lead the discussion. Start by asking them what they have heard. We run the risk of giving them more anxiety if we tell them things they aren't already thinking about.
- Let your children tell you about their specific worries and begin with these. Just being able to name their fears helps them.
- Always be honest and direct, yet age-appropriate. In other words, don't supply too much detail. Tell them only what they need to know.
- Focus on the helpers and all the good they are doing. Help your children figure out how to contribute to the good.
- Remind your children that God is in control. We receive each new day as a gift from Him, knowing that He has gone ahead of us into it and will help us with

---

56 Maxine Hancock, *People in Process—The Preschool Years: How to Develop Confidence, Character, and Creativity in Your Children* (Old Tappan, NJ: Fleming H. Revell, 1973), 31.

it. At night, we give our day back to God, trusting Him with tomorrow.[57]

---

[57] Sally Lloyd-Jones, "Helping Children with Scary News," *Sally Lloyd-Jones*. March 4, 2020 (https://www.sallylloyd-jones.com/helping-children-with-scary-news).

When a Child Wants to Be Baptized
Appendix 7

Most often, a child's parent will let the teacher or pastor know that their child wants to be baptized. Sometimes it's the parent who wants this for their child.

But whether it's the child wanting to be baptized or the parent urging their child in that direction, it's important to have a couple of sessions with the child—and ideally, the parent and child together. The parent will benefit from the teaching, too, gaining insight into their child's faith and becoming better equipped to nurture it. The entire experience will be enriched if during the sessions you give the parent an opportunity to talk about their own relationship with God.

If at any point it becomes clear to you that baptism for the child is the parent's choice and not the child's, explain to the parent that it's important to wait until the child expresses their own desire to be baptized.

The goals of the first session are to determine whether or not the child truly wants to be baptized—and if so, why. A child's understanding of Jesus as Saviour and Lord may seem inadequate to us, but if the child's faith is real, the desire to be baptized sincere, and their reason for wanting to be baptized sound, we shouldn't discourage them, delay them, or otherwise stand in their way. Jesus has said, *"Let the little children come to me, and do not hinder them"* (Matthew 19:14, Mark 10:14, Luke 18:16).

My pastor husband often explains that our journey toward God begins and continues with giving everything we know about ourselves to everything we know about God. Everything the child knows about themself and everything they know about God will, by God's grace, continually expand.

The following discussion guide will both give you insight into the child's faith and understanding and help the child grow in faith and understanding during the time you spend with them. Use the outline only as a guide. Keep truth simple. Stay free of dogma and rote answers. Keep your heart open to the witness of God's Spirit regarding the precious child He has brought to you.

If at the end of the first session, you have discerned that the child has a sincere faith and desire for God, arrange to meet with the child and/or child and parent a second time. The second session will focus more on the meaning and act of baptism.[58]

Session One: Exploring the Child's Faith and Understanding of the Gospel

Before you begin, find children's Bibles to use, one for each person participating. Help the child look up a few key verses as you go along. Find the verse first yourself and then give the child the page number.

1. **Break the ice.** Spend some time chatting to get acquainted or caught up.
2. **God.** Ask: "What do you think is the best thing about God?" Answers might include:
   - He created everything (Genesis 1:1).
   - He is Spirit (John 4:24).
   - He is eternal (Psalm 90:2).
   - He never changes (Malachi 3:6).
   - He is all-powerful (Matthew 19:26).

---

58 I based these sessions on Laurie Donahue and Ralph Rittenhouse's children's workbook, God....Should I be Baptized? (Somis CA: Lifesong Publishers, 2014).

- He knows everything, even our secrets (Psalm 139:1–4).
- He is everywhere (Jeremiah 23:24).
- He is faithful (1 Corinthians 1:9).
- He is holy (Leviticus 19:2).
- He is fair and just (Deuteronomy 32:4).
- He is love (1 John 4:8).

3. **Sin.** Ask: "What is sin?" Explain: "Sin is not obeying God. Sin is doing what is wrong and not doing what is right. Everyone sins." Look up: Romans 3:23 (*"... for all have sinned and fall short of the glory of God..."*).

    Ask: "How did sin happen?" Explain: "God's creation was perfect in the beginning. Then Adam and Eve used their free will to disobey God. Everyone since Adam and Eve has been born with sin or disobedience toward God in their hearts.

    Ask: "Why is sin a problem?" Explain: "Sin messes everything up—creation, people, relationships. Most sadly and importantly of all, it messes up a person's relationship with God and keeps them from being close to God."

    Ask: "What has to happen because of sin?" Explain: "Because sin is wrong, people must be punished for their sin. Romans 6:23 says that the punishment for sin is to die the kind of death that separates us from God forever. But God loves us too much to want this to happen to us. He wants us close to Him. So God made a way for our sins to be forgiven or wiped away." Look up: Romans 6:23 (*"For the wages of sin is death, but the gift of God is eternal life in Christ Jesus our Lord"*).

4. **Jesus.** Ask: "Who is Jesus? What is the most important thing Jesus did for us?" Explain: "God sent His perfect Son Jesus into the world. Jesus had no sin of His own that needed to be punished. Because Jesus loves us so much, He stepped into our place and died the death we deserve when He died on the cross. Because Jesus has died for our sins, God will forgive us."

Illustrate: Pretend you messed up, did something wrong, and had to be punished, but someone else stepped in and took your punishment. What is something you could have done wrong? What might your punishment be? Who would love you enough to step into your place and take your punishment for you? If that happened, how would it make you feel?

Look up: 1 Corinthians 15:3–4 (*"For what I received I passed on to you as of first importance: that Christ died for our sins according to the Scriptures, that he was buried, that he was raised on the third day according to the Scriptures..."*). Explain: "This verse tells us that after Jesus died for us, He came alive again. We celebrate the fact that Jesus died and came alive again at Easter."

Look up: Colossians 2:13 (*"When you were dead in your sins and in the uncircumcision of your flesh, God made you alive with Christ. He forgave us all our sins..."*). Explain: "This verse tells us that because Jesus died in our place, God will forgive all our sins and give us a new forgiven life."

Look up: Isaiah 1:18 (*"Though your sins are like scarlet, they shall be as white as snow"*). Explain: "When God forgives our sins, He makes our hearts clean, as though our sins were never even there. Imagine your heart being dark with sin. God says that when He forgives us, He washes all the dark away and makes our hearts as clean as fresh fallen snow."

5. **Acceptance.** Explain: "Jesus's death on the cross, and God's forgiveness because of what Jesus did for us, is a gift God wants to give everyone, but no one has this gift until they accept it from God."

   Illustrate: Begin to hand the child an item. Extend your arms toward the child, but pause with the item in your hands. Show the child that it is not theirs and can't be theirs until they take it from you.

   Ask: "How do we receive or accept from God the gift of forgiveness He wants to give us through Jesus's death?" Explain: "We can only receive it by believing in it."

   Look up: Ephesians 2:8–9 (*"For it is by grace you have been saved, through faith—and this is not from yourselves, it is the gift of God—not by works, so that no one can boast"*). Look up: John 1:12 (*"Yet to all who did receive him, to those who believed in his name, he gave the right to become children of God..."*). Look up: John 3:16 (*"For God so loved the world that he gave his one and only Son, that whoever believes in him shall not perish but have eternal life"*).

6. **Eternal life.** Ask: "What is eternal life?" Explain: "The word eternal means 'forever.' It's something that never ends. Eternal life is life lived close to God now and forever in heaven with Him when our life on earth is done. Someday our bodies will wear out and die, but the real us inside—the real you inside your body, the part of you that loves ice cream and your mom—will live forever with God when you receive the gift of what Jesus did for you."

Look up: John 14:6 (*"Jesus answered, 'I am the way and the truth and the life. No one comes to the Father except through me'"*). Explain: "Jesus says very clearly that the only way to be close to God now and forever in heaven is to believe in Jesus and in all He did for us when He died on the cross and then came alive again."

7. **A Gospel illustration.** At this point, you may want to review the main points of the Gospel with a visual.

8. **Decision.** Ask: "Have you ever thanked God for Jesus's death on the cross? Have you thanked God for forgiving you because of Jesus's death? Have you given your life to Jesus so He can lead it?"

    Ask: "Would you like to pray and talk to God about this now?" Explain: "You can talk to God with your own words, or you can pray this prayer out loud or in your heart: 'Dear God, thank You for loving me so much that You sent Jesus, Your Son, to die for me. I am sorry for all the times I have not obeyed You. Thank You that Jesus died on the cross to pay for my sins. Thank You that You forgive me and that I will live forever with You because of what Jesus has done for me. I want to obey You. Please come into my life and lead it.'"

Session Two: Baptism and Beyond

1. **The Gospel.** Give the child the Gospel visual you showed them in your first session. Ask them to use it to explain the Gospel to you. Don't expect a perfect presentation! Celebrate the parts that the child understands. Review the parts that seem vague.

2. **Baptism.** Explain that when we get baptized, the person who baptizes us lays us backward into the water and then lifts us up again. Demonstrate this with a doll and/or imaginary water.
3. **Why?** Ask: "Why do people get baptized?" Explain: "To show that they believe in Jesus and what He did for them when He died on the cross. To show they want to follow Jesus. To give a picture of Jesus's death and resurrection. To give a picture of what has happened inside them because they believe in Jesus. Their old sinful life is gone. A new life with Jesus has begun. To show that God has forgiven their sins or washed them away. To obey God. Jesus wants His followers to be baptized."

    Look up: Matthew 28:18–20 (*"Then Jesus came to them and said, 'All authority in heaven and on earth has been given to me. Therefore go and make disciples of all nations, baptizing them in the name of the Father and of the Son and of the Holy Spirit, and teaching them to obey everything I have commanded you. And surely I am with you always, to the very end of the age'"*). There are also several examples of believers being baptized in Acts (2:41, 8:12–13, 8:38, 9:18, 10:48, 16:15, 16:33, 18:8, 19:5) Jesus Himself was baptized by John the Baptist to show that is something He wants His followers to do (Mark 1: 9–11).
4. **How?** Ask: "How are we baptized?" Explain: "The Greek word *baptizo* means 'to dip or to wash.' Jesus and others we read about in the Bible went down into the water, were immersed in the water, and then were brought back up again. Baptism is a picture of Jesus's death and resurrection. Being put into the water is like Jesus's body being put into the ground, and being

lifted up out of the water is like Jesus coming alive again. In the same way, it is a picture of what happens inside us when we believe in Jesus. Our old sinful self dies (we are buried in the water). Jesus comes into our life to make it new (we are lifted up out of the water). Baptism is also a picture of God forgiving, or washing away, our sins because of our faith in Jesus. Being put into the water and being brought back up out of it is like having our sins washed away."

5. **Who?** Ask: "Who should be baptized?" Explain: "Only those who believe in Jesus and want to follow Him."

    Ask: "What does it mean to follow Jesus?" Explain: "To follow Jesus means to obey His teachings and follow His example. It also means to let Him lead our lives."

    Look up: 1 John 2:3, 5–6 (*"We know that we have come to know him if we keep his commands... This is how we know we are in him: Whoever claims to live in him must live as Jesus did"*).

6. **The Holy Spirit.** Explain: "Jesus doesn't want or expect us to obey Him and follow His example on our own. He gives every believer His Holy Spirit to help them. This is how Jesus lives in our hearts. His body doesn't climb into our bodies and live in our tummies. He comes in His Spirit to live in our hearts. God's Spirit inside of us is powerful enough to help us with everything He wants us to be and do."

    Look up: Ephesians 3:20 (*"Now to him who is able to do immeasurably more than all we ask or imagine, according to his power that is at work within us..."*).

Explain: "God helps us with His Holy Spirit when we stay close to God in prayer, ask God for His help, and trust God for the help we need. Even though we have God's Holy Spirit inside of us, because we are still human we will continue to make mistakes and disobey God. But Jesus died for these sins, too. God has promised that whenever we admit or confess that we have sinned, and ask Him to forgive us, He will."

Look up: 1 John 1:9 (*"If we confess our sins, he is faithful and just and will forgive us our sins and purify us from all unrighteousness"*).

7. **After baptism.** Ask: "What are some of the things God has given us to help us stay close to Him, trust Him for help, and follow Jesus?" Explain: "God has given us prayer. We can talk with God about anything, anytime, anywhere. In fact, God wants us to be praying simple prayers for His help all the time!"

Look up: 1 Thessalonians 5:17 (*"...pray continually..."*).

Explain: "God has given us His Word, the Bible. God wants us to read His Word, think about it, and pray about it every day."

Look up: Joshua 1:8 (*"Keep this Book of the Law always on your lips; meditate on it day and night, so that you may be careful to do everything written in it. Then you will be prosperous and successful"*).

Explain: "There are some great devotional books for kids that can help you with this. If you want to read the Bible on your own, the best place to start is by reading about Jesus in either the Gospel of John or the Gospel of Mark." Consider gifting the child with their own Bible and/or a daily devotions guide when they are baptized.

Explain: "God has given us other believers and He wants us to help each other. He wants us to gather regularly to worship Him, pray, and study His Word. It is important to go to church to be with other believers every week."

Look up: Hebrews 10:25 ("...*not giving up meeting together, as some are in the habit of doing, but encouraging one another—and all the more as you see the Day approaching*").

8. **Telling others.** Explain: "God wants us to tell others about Jesus the way Andrew did!"

Look up: John 1:41–42 ("*The first thing Andrew did was to find his brother Simon and tell him, 'We have found the Messiah' (that is, the Christ). And he brought him to Jesus*"). Ask: "What do you want to tell others about Jesus? Who will you tell?"

9. **Communion.** Explain: "One way we can tell others that we love and follow Jesus is to participate in communion. Like baptism, communion is a picture of Jesus. The broken bread we eat at communion is a symbol of Jesus's body. It shows that Jesus died a difficult death for us. The red juice is a symbol of Jesus's blood. It shows that Jesus died a sacrificial death for us. The word 'sacrificial' means that Jesus died so we can live. As we look at the bread and the juice, we thank Jesus for dying for us. We feel sad if we haven't been showing Him that we love Him. We ask Him to forgive us and help us do better. When we eat the bread and drink the juice, we remember that God loves us very much indeed. We remember that God sent His Son Jesus to die for us so we can be forgiven

by God and live close to Him forever. We feel glad. Our hearts are filled with love and thanks to God for Jesus. When we eat the bread and drink the juice, we show everyone that we believe in Jesus. We eat the bread and drink the juice with other believers to show that we all belong to Jesus, and that because we all belong to Jesus we belong to one another, too."

10. **Preparation.** You will want to explain to the child exactly how you will baptize them—where they will stand in the water, how you will support them, how to plug their nose and bend their knees, what you will ask them and how they will respond, etc.

In one of our churches, we placed a cement block on the floor of our baptism tank to lift children above the wall of the tank so people could see them. If you make similar arrangements, make sure that the cement block is wrapped well with a thick towel. Stubbing a toe can hurt!

Show the child the baptism tank or arrange to show it to them later.

Explain to the child what they are to wear into the water. Ask them to bring towels, hairbrush, and a change of clothes.

If the child is expected to share their faith story at their baptism, you may want to make notes for them while they share their story with you. Or give them a set of questions to help them prepare their story. For example, "When did you first start to love and trust Jesus? What do you love most about Jesus? Why did Jesus die on the cross? How does God help you? What do you thank God for and why? Why do you want to be baptized?"

The child may want to ask someone who has played a significant role in their journey to and with Jesus to read their story just before they are baptized.

If the child needs to be interviewed by your deacons or other church leaders, arrange the interview. Have the child prepare their faith story for the interview.

Explain to the child that after they are baptized, they will be given the opportunity to join the church. Tell them how this will happen and when.

Connect the child with an older person in your church who will pray for them and help them nurture their relationship with God.

Recommended Resources
Appendix 8

Welcome

- Gospel Light Sunday School Curriculum: Baby Beginnings Nursery Kit (https://www.christianbook.com/page/sunday-school-curriculum/gospel-light-sunday-school/gl-curriculum). This curriculum provides great ideas for learning through play.
- Shirley K. Morgenthaler, *Right from the Start: A Parent's Guide to the Young Child's Faith Development* (St. Louis, MO: Concordia Publishing House, 2001). This book provides helpful insights for parents and teachers.

Wonder

- Paul J. Loth, *First Steps: 75 Devotions for Families with Young Children*, Daniel J. Hochstatter, ill. (Nashville, TN: Thomas Nelson, 1992). These brief, age-appropriate devotions follow the four-step Hook/Book/Look/Took outline of an effective Bible lesson.
- Gospel Light Sunday School Curriculum: Preschool to Ages 4–5 (https://www.christianbook.com/page/sunday-school-curriculum/gospel-light-sunday-school/gl-curriculum). In this curriculum, the Bible stories are short and simple. There are large, brightly coloured flannelgraph visuals for every story.

Gospel Light also produces children's songs that match preschool teaching themes and provides these on reproducible CDs, with one music CD per teaching kit. Additional visuals include bright, "talk about" picture posters.

Each lesson includes a variety of learning activities that maximize learning by engaging a young child's five senses. Each lesson includes lots of learning through play ideas. Each lesson appeals to a young child's highly imaginative love of puppets by including a simple puppet script.

Every Gospel Light Preschool Kit includes thirteen lessons and enough activity and take-home pages for ten children. Together, the four seasons of Gospel Light Preschool Curriculum (Winter, Spring, Summer, and Fall) cover both Old Testament stories and New Testament stories, including Jesus's birth, life, death, and resurrection.

Gospel Light produces preschool curricula for ages two to three as well, but it's usually easier to simplify ideas for younger children than expand them for older children.

- Karyn Henley, *The Beginner's Bible*, Dennas Davis, ill. (Grand Rapids, MI: Zondervan, 2016). The stories in this Bible are brief, unembellished, and illustrated with uncluttered, brightly coloured pictures. This publication not only includes appropriate Bible stories for young children, but it also presents them in biblical sequence!

Recommended Resources

Discover

- Betty Lukens (www.bettylukens.com). Visit this site for felt visuals and boards for Bible stories. Despite our media-saturated age, felt visuals intrigue today's preschool and early elementary children. A few decades ago, the flannelgraph method of storytelling was used so incessantly that it lost its appeal, but felt visuals are fresh and new for today's kids. Children love watching us change them as we tell the story, and they love changing them as they retell the story!
- CBM Kids Care (https://kidscare.cbmin.org). This site, produced by Canadian Baptist Ministries, provides mission lessons for children.
- Judy Capehart, Gordon West, and Becki West, *The Discipline Guide for Children's Ministry* (Loveland, CO: Group, 1997). This book offers many easy-to-read practical suggestions for effectively disciplining children.
- Sally Lloyd-Jones, *The Jesus Storybook Bible* (Grand Rapids, MI: Zondervan, 2007). This book is beautifully and refreshingly written, presenting the Bible as one story.

Launch

- CPYU's Digital Kids Initiative (https://digitalkidsinitiative.com). This site offers help for parents and other adults who need to talk with kids about pornography, teen depression, and other challenging topics.

- *The Hands-On Bible* (Carol Stream, IL: Tyndale House, 2010). This is an easy-to-read version of the Bible for older elementary school children.
- Dave and Neta Jackson, *Hero Tales* (Minneapolis, MN: Bethany House, 1996, 1997). This title is presented as two volumes, with thirty short biographical narratives written for children. Read the life stories of faith heroes like Harriet Tubman, J. Hudson Taylor, William and Catherine Booth, Corrie ten Boom, and others with your child. Talk about them together.
- *The Wonder Devotional, Book One: Daily Adventures with God* (Warrenton, MO: Child Evangelism Fellowship, 2001). This book presents sound, practical, and concise theology for kids in either one volume or soft-covered booklets of sixty devotions each.

Safety on the Trail

- "Reducing the Risk," a child protection training manual and DVD series produced by *Christianity Today*. This resource is so titled because, as the writers point out, we can never guarantee the absolute safety of any environment. However, every piece of sound protection policy that is put in place makes it less likely that anything inappropriate will occur.

Parents on the Trail

- Chip Ingram, *Effective Parenting in a Defective World: How to Raise Kids who Stand Out from the Crowd* (Carol Stream, IL: Tyndale House, 2006).

- Mark Holman, *Faith Begins at Home: The Family Makeover with Christ at the Center* (Ventura, CA: Regal Books, 2005). This book includes small group discussion starters.
- John Trent and Jane Vogel, *Faith Launch: A Simple Plan to Ignite Your Child's Love for Jesus* (Carol Stream, IL: Tyndale House, 2008). This book includes thirteen weeks of spiritual formation lesson plans and responses to faith questions children ask.
- Dr. Tim Kimmel, *Grace-Based Parenting: Set Your Family Free* (Nashville, TN: Thomas Nelson, 2004). This book includes discussion questions.
- Dr. Tim Kimmel, Raising Kids Who Turn Out Right: Focusing on What Really Matters (Scottsdale, AZ: Family Matters, 2005).
- Reggie Joiner and Carey Nieuwhof, *Parenting Beyond Your Capacity; Connect Your Family to a Wider World* (Colorado Springs, CO: David C. Cook, 2010).
- Grant Edwards, *Passing the Baton: Guide Your Child to Follow Jesus* (Loveland, CO: Group, 2009). This book includes ten weeks of activities and conversations you can share with your child.
- Jan Rigby, *Raising Unselfish Children in a Self-Absorbed World* (New York, NY: Howard Books, 2008).
- Michelle Anthony, *Spiritual Parenting: An Awakening for Today's Families* (Colorado Springs, CO: David C. Cook, 2010).
- Gary Chapman and Ross Campbell, *The Five Love Languages of Children* (Chicago, IL: Northfield Publishing, 2005).
- Stormie Omartian, *The Power of a Praying Parent* (Eugene, OR: Harvest House Publishers, 2005).

- George Barna, *Transforming Children into Spiritual Champions: Why Children Should Be Your Church's #1 Priority* (Ventura, CA: Regal Books, 2004). This is a key read for parents as well as church leaders.

Partners on the Trail

- Mark Holman, *Building Faith at Home: Why Faith at Home Must Be Your Church's #1 Priority* (Ventura, CA: Regal Books, 2007).
- Brian Haynes, *Shift: What It Takes to Finally Reach Families Today* (Loveland, CO: Group, 2009).
- Reggie Joiner, *Think Orange: Imagine the Impact When Church and Family Collide* (Colorado Springs, CO: David C. Cook, 2009).
- George Barna, *Transforming Children into Spiritual Champions: Why Children Should Be Your Church's #1 Priority* (Ventura, CA: Regal Books, 2003). This is a key read for parents as well as church leaders.

Digital Expressions of The Trail

- The Bible App for Kids (https://bibleappforkids.com). This downloadable app is designed to help kids explore the Bible. It's aimed at those in preschool or Kindergarten.
- Playlists for Personalized Faith Formation (https://www.lifelongfaith.com/playlists.html). This excellent website offers a video presentation to help us understand what faith formation playlists are, why we should use them, and tips for creating them for your ministry.

- Digital Learning Apps (https://www.lifelongfaith.com/learning-apps.html). This site presents a list and description of the best online apps available for assisting with digital faith formation.
- Andrae Jones, "Implementing Digital Discipleship for Kids," *Orange Kids*. Date of access: May 13, 2022 (https://orangekidmin.com/implementing-digital-discipleship-for-kids). This short article from a church leader is about implementing a plan for digital discipleship.
- Parent Cue (https://theparentcue.org). This site offers articles and resources for parents, as well as a downloadable app that prompts regular devotion, discussion, and prayer times for families.
- Parenting for Faith (https://www.parentingforfaith.brf.org.uk). This site presents online video training available for free, including a leader handbook and participant material. There are also options to join in regular parent Facebook chats and listen to podcasts on various parenting issues.
- Saddleback Kids Church at Home (http://www.saddlebackkids.com/church-at-home/). This site offers online video teachings for different age groups, complete with parent resources such as downloadable activity sheets.
- Superbook (https://www.superbookproject.com). This is a website and app for digital evangelism and discipleship of kids. It includes videos, challenges, and games.
- Brittany Nelson, "Three Reasons Why Children's Ministry Leaders Must Embrace Digital Discipleship," *Deeper Kidmin*. March 31, 2021 (https://

deeperkidmin.com/why-childrens-ministry-leaders-must-embrace-digital-discipleship). This article provides some key reasons why digital discipleship is important. It's the first in a series of practical resources, ideas, and suggestions for implementing and running a digital children's ministry. Further resources include online training.

Grandparents on the Trail

- Kay Swatkowski, *A Grandmother's Prayers: 60 Days of Devotions and Prayer* (Grand Rapids, MI: Discovery House, 2015).
- Dr. Tim and Darcey Kimmel, *Extreme Grandparenting* (Carol Stream, IL: Tyndale House, 2007).
- Janet Teitsort, *Long Distance Grandma: Staying Connected Across the Miles* (Brentwood, TN: Howard Books, 2005).
- Eric Wiggin, *The Gift of Grandparenting* (Wheaton, IL: Tyndale House, 2001).
- Stormie Omartian, *The Power of Praying for Your Adult Children* (Eugene, OR: Harvest House, 2009).

Immersing the Trail in Intergenerational Ministry

Books

- Lucy Moore, *All-Age Worship* (Oxford, UK: The Bible Reading Fellowship, 2016).
- Cory Seibel, ed., *Engage All Generations: A Strategic Toolkit for Creating Intergenerational Faith Communities* (Abilene, TX: Abilene Christian University Press,

2021). This book was produced from the second Intergenerate conference held in 2019.

- Holly Catterton Allen, *Intergenerate: Transforming Churches through Intergenerational Ministry* (Abilene, TX: Abilene Christian University Press, 2018). This book was produced from the first Intergenerate conference. It includes some academic research in addition to ideas for incorporating intergenerational ministry.
- Holly Allen and Christine Stonehouse, *Intergenerational Christian Formation: Bringing the Whole Church in Ministry, Community and Worship* (Westmont, IL: InterVarsity Press, 2012). This is a foundational text on intergenerational Christian formation that provides background, theory, and theology as well as some ideas for incorporating intergenerational ministry in different ways.
- Lucy Moore and Jane Leadbetter, *Messy Church: Fresh Ideas for building a Christ-Centered Community* (Westmont, IL: InterVarsity Press, 2017).
- Ally Barrett, *Preaching with All Ages: Twelve Steps to Grow Your Skills and Confidence* (Norwich, UK: Canterbury Press, 2019). This book has some good pointers for writing a sermon for multi-age groups.
- Peter Menconi, *The Intergenerational Church* (London, UK: Sage Publishing, 2010).

Websites

- Intergenerate is a conference that combines both academic and practical speakers, presentations, and workshops (http://www.intergenerateconference.com).

- Faith Formation Ministries, "Ten Ways to Be A More Intergenerational Church," *Network*. June 6, 2018 (https://network.crcna.org/faith-nurture/how-become-more-intergenerational-church).
- Brad M. Griffin, "Intergenerational Ministry Beyond the Rhetoric," *Fuller Youth Institute*. April 4, 2011 (https://fulleryouthinstitute.org/blog/intergenerational-ministry-beyond-the-rhetoric).

Helping Parents Nurture Good Relationships with Their Children
Appendix 6

- Randy Alcorn, *Heaven for Kids: Answers Kids Will Understand* (Carol Stream, IL: Tyndale House, 2006). This book is based on the author's bestselling book for adults, *Heaven*.
- Hillary Morgan Ferrer, ed., *Mama Bear Apologetics: Empowering Your Kids to Challenge Cultural Lies* (Eugene, OR: Harvest House, 2019). I wish I had read this book when we were raising our children!
- *801 Questions Kids Ask About God: With Answers from the Bible* (Carol Stream, IL: Tyndale House, 2000).

When a Child Wants to Be Baptized
Appendix 7

- Laurie Donahue and Ralph Rittenhouse, *God... Should I Be Baptized?* (Somis, CA: LifeSong Publishers, 2014). This is a handbook for kids between the ages of eight and twelve. You may want to work through the actual book with the child session by

session, give the child the book to work through at home, or use the book as I have done, for reference.
- "The Bridge to Life Illustration," *Navigators Discipleship*. Date of access: May 13, 2022 (https://www.navigators.org/wp-content/uploads/2021/02/navigators-bridge-to-life.pdf).
- *The Wonder Devotional, Book One: Daily Adventures with God* (Warrenton, MO: Child Evangelism Fellowship, 2001).
- Jennifer Hooks, *365 Devotions for Kids* (Loveland, CO: Group, 2018). This is a daily devotional book for kids that complements *The Hands-On Bible*.

Bibliography

Books

Allen, Holly Catterton (ED), *Nurturing Children's Spirituality; Christian Perspectives and Best Practices* (Eugene, OR: Cascade Books, 2008).

Anthony, Michelle, *Spiritual Parenting: An Awakening for Today's Parents* (Colorado Springs, CO: David C. Cook, 2010).

Barna, George, *Transforming Children into Spiritual Champions: Why Children Should Be Your Church's #1 Priority* (Ventura, CA: Regal Books, 2003).

Capehart, Judy, Gordon West and Becki West, *The Discipline Guide for Children's Ministry* (Loveland, CO: Group, 1997).

Carr, Jo and Imogene Sorley, *The Intentional Family* (Nashville, TN: Abingdon Press, 1971).

Donahue, Laurie and Ralph Rittenhouse, *God... Should I Be Baptized?* (Somis, CA: LifeSong Publishers, 2014).

Hancock, Maxine, *People in Process—The Preschool Years: How to Develop Confidence, Character, and Creativity in Your Children* (Old Tappan, NJ: Fleming H. Revell, 1973).

Hayes, Brian, *Shift: What It Takes to Finally Reach Families Today* (Loveland, CO: Group, 2009).

Holman, Mark, *Faith Begins at Home: The Family Makeover with Christ at the Center* (Ventura, CA: Regal Books, 2005).

Joiner, Reggie, *Think Orange: Imagine the Impact When Church and Family Collide* (Colorado Springs, CO: David C. Cook, 2009).

Joiner, Reggie and Carey Nieuwhof, *Parenting Beyond Your Capacity: Connect Your Family to a Wider Community* (Colorado Springs, CO: David C. Cook, 2010).

Kimmel, Dr. Tim and Darcey, *Extreme Grandparenting* (Carol Stream, IL: Tyndale House, 2007).

Klumpenhower, Jack, *Show Them Jesus: Teaching the Gospel to Kids* (Greensboro, NC: New Growth Press, 2017).

Morgenthaler, Shirley. *Right from the Start: A Parent's Guide to the Young Child's Faith Development* (St. Louis, MO: Concordia Publishing House, 2001).

Mullholland, M. Robert Jr., *Invitation to a Journey: A Road Map for Spiritual Formation* (Downers Grove, IL: InterVarsity Press, 2016).

Peterson, Eugene, *A Long Obedience in the Same Direction: Discipleship in an Instant Society* (Downers Grove, IL: InterVarsity Press, 2021).

"Reducing the Risk" (Carol Stream, IL: Christianity Today, 2003).

Richards, Lawrence O., *A Theology of Children's Ministry* (Grand Rapids, MI: Zondervan, 1983).

Richards, Lawrence O., *Creative Bible Teaching* (Chicago, IL: Moody Press, 1970).

Richards, Lawrence O., *Youth Ministry: Its Renewal in the Local Church* (Grand Rapids, MI: Zondervan, 1972).

Trent, John and Jane Vogel, *Faith Launch: A Simple Plan to Ignite Your Child's Love for Jesus* (Carol Stream, IL: Tyndale House, 2008).

Articles and Blogs

Bastian, Karl, "Make 'Em Laugh," *Children's Ministry Magazine*, January-February 2017.

Burns, Jim, "Who We Are," *Thriving Family*, January-February 2013.

Lloyd-Jones, Sally, "Helping Children with Scary News," *Sally Lloyd-Jones*. March 4, 2020 (https://www.sallylloyd-jones.com/helping-children-with-scary-news).

Roberto, John, "Our Future Is Intergenerational," *Christian Education Journal*, series 3, volume 9, number 1, 2012.

Snider, Emily, "Mindfulness," *Children's Ministry Magazine*, January-February 2017.

Schweikert, GiGi, "3–5 Age Level Insights," *Children's Ministry Magazine*, July-August 2011.

www.ingramcontent.com/pod-product-compliance
Lightning Source LLC
Chambersburg PA
CBHW071741150426
43191CB00010B/1652